WHEN THE OCEAN ROARED

My Mother's Murder
and other Childhood Memories

By
Anne Steinle

To Anne

May your mind be open and kindness be your guide!

Love
Anne

ISBN 9798553851460

Young Water Babies

i

TABLE OF CONTENTS

Section Six

Section Seven

Section Eight

Section Nine

Section Ten

Section Eleven

Section Twelve

Epilogue

About the Author

INTRODUCTION

It seems common for kids not to know their parents as the individuals they were before they were married, before they were settled. It may be in the parent handbook not to let your children know so much of your younger antics, possibly to retain a bit of dignity and/or control. But me not having raised a child, I thought my niece and nephew might like to know a bit more about their Grandmother and her children, their Aunt and Father, and what shaped them into the adults they came to be. It's not always a pretty story, but if you look into anyone's past there will be something trying to slither its way out from under that big rock.

Stephan

As a first time writer, I hope you find this entertaining, perhaps a little thought provoking or even insightful here and there. I'm sure there will be boring parts (one friend said I should have included some sex stories...the next book). I have always found personality quirks and bents endearing (or disturbing in some cases), so I probably spent too much time describing them, but I think it's important to notice all you can about a person. This is written chronologically as I wanted to show the 'Before' and 'After' (as I refer to it throughout the book) of my Mother's murder. Forgive me if I go a bit long in the 'Before'. These are the only memories of my Mother and reliving so many of them have made these past few winters considerably warmer.

Elizabeth

Something learned during this five year process was that too many people my age do not remember much about their childhood. How sad to forget the exhilaration of discovering a nest of baby garter snakes or the feeling of freedom that bell gave you at the end of the school day. The freedom in general. Few fears and no financial burdens. The questioning and curiosity of everything. Evvverything! A day when people just Give you Candy! And oh my God, CHRISTMAS! Will it EVER get here!

That is of course, if you were lucky enough to have such a childhood. The world starts its random squashing of dreams mighty early sometimes. To balance with hope, that early squashing often pushes out some bigger and brighter dreams later on in life. In any case, I was lucky enough for a while to live like the happy-go-lucky sit-com actors I was watching on TV, or at least to have a Mother who made me feel as though I was.

It's been 50 years since my Mother's murder. Obviously, I could have handled things differently, better, in those early years, but I have long since found my peace. I'm fully aware of the things missing in my life which is why I cherish what I do have. There are many friends I can count on and delight in being around. My work is a huge creative outlet not to mention the social aspects; client/friends all over town and the deep personal conversations that happen in the safe space of my little downtown shop. My country home life is simply glorious and I cannot begin to describe the joy my gardens bring me (although I try later in the book). I tend to 'feel the moment' by living in the present and say an appreciative "Thank You" out loud when things go well, knowing that the opposite lurks right around the corner. The absolute luxury of a hot shower, the 'magic' of positive thought, laughing uncontrollably…such joys are not to be taken for granted.

I do find the disconnection with our natural surroundings unsettling, to say the least. The significance of the environment is becoming something that must be learned rather than instinctively felt. We egotistically put ourselves above the very things that offer their rich life giving properties. Even the quality of our air and water are being brushed aside as trivial in our increasingly sterile atmospheres.

Thankfully some eyes are open and there are pockets of progress being made toward keeping the intricate weave of the ecosystem intact, providing some hope for a pleasant life in the future, or rather life at all. Unfortunately, the blinding shimmer of gold and all its so called glories seem to get in the way of that progress far too often. What good is money if you can't breathe?

It boils down to this:

Humans Gone, Nature Lives On. Nature Gone, Humans Gone.

We Need It, It Doesn't Need Us.

The world will continue to be a beautiful and ugly place at the same time. Yes, there is gloom and doom, but there is also light and life. Which would you rather have as a surround? And to help someone born into a world without that choice should not be a passing thought.

Well, I've managed to digress before I've even started. There will be a lot of that no doubt. Anyway, this book is about both happy and tragic times and the people who have shared them with me. I hope you enjoy reading it as much as I've enjoyed writing it.

1000 B.C.

Fantastic is the word to describe my childhood. Grandparent types were everywhere, the Earth itself provided endless entertainment and new groups of kids would periodically appear for us to romp around with. My Mother and older brother Bob were both my best friends and heroes. We had food every day, different clothes for each school year and a few new toys every Christmas. A huge cat who earned the name Sandy by disappearing into the road out front lived with us and eventually the greatest dog in the world came barreling into our lives. Rich fodder for a chunky little tomboy with a hearty appetite and boundless energy.

In hindsight, Mother may have seen us a little differently. She was a recent widow with two young children, full blown Parkinson's disease and missing a lung from tuberculosis in her teens. Her husband of not even ten years had suddenly died of an aneurism at age 41. This was before their newest investment plans had time to get a foothold and now she was left alone and with only his $3000.00 a year Social Security to support the family. Part of their plan involved building houses and the neighborhood they'd picked to start out in was a lovely kid friendly retirement village. She did have friends to rely on in emergency, but the day to day duties were now all on her weakening shoulders. She was independent in her thinking, fair and just, possessed abundant common sense to help her with the scam artists of the world and generally as smart as a whip. Her breathing seemed to pose no problem, but this Parkinson's business was really slowing her down. Perhaps the 'Easier Street' she was looking forward to living on now appeared to be a few roads over.

Bob may have been looking through a darker lens as well. Until our Dad died, his view of the Shangri-La they had moved to was similar to mine. But after his death, Bob was being told things like "Looks like you're the man of the family now", "You've been handed the reins boy" and "You're going to have to step up to the plate son". Not from Mother of course, from well-wishers and family friends. He was a smart boy, would later score a high genius I.Q. in fact, but he didn't know much about his father's career of architecture and electrical engineering or even how to drive a car. No matter, his Mother and little sister needed him. Suddenly responsibilities of grand proportion had fallen into his worried little lap and he took them seriously.

>>

My parents and toddler Bob had moved to central Florida in the 1950's after accepting the fact that a previous investment plan was not going to work out. Along with my Aunt Dolores and Dad's brother Frank, they had followed a current trend by pulling up their Brooklyn stakes to start a mink farm. Choosing the crossroads town of Catawissa, Mo. they worked at it long enough for Bob to be conceived, born and poop his diapers for a good year. In a selfish thought I am eternally grateful for that small failure in their lives as I am the flipside of what I envision a mink heiress to be. And I quake in my shoes when imagining my after school clean up chores. Do you know that only the center back strip of fur is used? About two hundred animals die for the making of one coat!

Early May 1951 - Cattawisa. I love that my parents are dressed alike! Dolores always had Beagles.

I was told that the choices of where to move next had been whittled down to Dade City, Florida and somewhere in Hawaii. I'm guessing that the fantasy of island living was put on the back burner as practicality and child rearing won out. Dolores was soon to have her first born as well so if an argument even conspired, no doubt it was girls against boys or rather parents against dreamers.

But the decision was made and taken to heart by all. Frank and Dolores moved into the classic two bedroom cement block ranch in a middle class neighborhood in Dade City. Dolores had three boys and took care of everything on the home front. Sole breadwinner Frank got a job at the American Can factory connected to the juicing plant called Pasco Packing which provided the world with frozen concentrate. I doubt that this was his dream job but they were truly in love and made a happy and long lived life for themselves.

My parents chose Orange Grove Villa, built along Hwy 301 half way between Dade City and Zephyrhills and set in the middle of some stunning countryside. Dad lived long enough to finish two other houses besides our own, but cash flow along with many other things stopped when the builder did.

Mother proved her genius with stretching the dollar and with us adhering to her advice on taking care of what we had as "There Would Be No Replacement" we never felt without. Since I was only a year old when Dad died, I have no memory of him and for some odd reason no one ever talked about him. Maybe it was too painful. The only description I ever heard was that he was 'the nice one' of the three brothers. Frank was a loving and good man, but stern and more serious, and Uncle Bob remained in New York, was in advertising and died too early from alcoholism.

For the longest time the only photo I had of my Father was in a gold locket that flipped open to display tiny glimpses of four people. One was of him in a striped shirt with happiness on his face. It wasn't until I was in my forties that the larger picture developed when a boyfriend casually asked (for the first time in my life) which parent I favored. I was stunned by the question as reality came crashing in. I looked like my father! I had his smile, his two front teeth exactly. He and my Mother were a couple in love. He would have been at the dinner table and tucked me into bed at night. He'd carry me on his shoulders and play horsie with me. His safe hugs would have melted away the hurts of the world. He was my Daddy! I would have been Daddy's Little Girl. I cried for weeks after that revelation and still tear up when it hits me just right.

The initial unease I feel when meeting a man for the first time might be tempered had I grown up with my loving father but without that early blanket of safety, the disrespect I've encountered over the years, the condescending attitudes and quick dismissals, not to mention the wild anger and physical betrayals tend to stay a little sharper in focus. Don't get me wrong, I have many fine male friends and acquaintances and feel comfortable with men who pose no threat. It's the other smaller group that unfortunately casts that first dark shadow.

Another 'side effect' of my father dying early was that I was shown daily that a woman, even one with severe health issues, is a capable human being. I'm not a feminist because no wall was built needing to be toppled and equality was Never in question. 'Proving myself' doesn't apply. So when a man and the occasional woman treat me as an inferior, it's immediately noticeable and tiresome.

But back to earlier and more innocent days. Aside from our beloved trucks, baseball equipment, the stuffed animals and my Barbie ("A Barbie in every pot", right?), Bob and I had the world itself to play with. The field between our house and the highway was never mowed so it turned into a house or a fort, depending on mood, by rolling around and flattening out 'rooms'. As a house I'd bring out the little green bench my Dad had built and use it as a stove to cook mud pies. In the big yellow Pyrex bowl from that colorful set everyone owned, I'd collect as many different weed tops and leaves as I could find for the salad. We would usually end up eating most of each. With the blissful ignorance that helps children plow through life, we were fortifying our already strong constitutions. We were also lucky.

Then there was the monstrous male Mulberry tree in our front yard that I practically lived in. It had big wide branches to kick back and cloud watch and was sturdy throughout when the neighbor kids came to roost. The hole in the untamed back acre of our property had originally been dug as a burning pit, but Bob and I took it over immediately as the perfect place to crash our cars to then rescue with our cranes and tow trucks. We spent an enormous amount of time out there and always had a blast.

And of course, there were the orange groves that went up the hill after our little neighborhood roads dead ended. We were always racing around in there throwing and dodging rotten oranges. Being sticky was a way of life in the summer. Screams rang out when a kid got wrapped in a gigantic web woven by one of Florida's massive spiders. It was shrieks of laughter at the victim thrashing around trying to find the spider that was no doubt delivering a thousand babies somewhere on him; shrieks of terror from the one caught.

We were also gifted a little patch of woods for other kinds of adventures. Fallen trees housed snakes, roaches and other ickmonsters to be deemed 'down the shirt' worthy. The long gray Spanish moss (loaded with little red ticks) hung thick from the branches making for great beards and wigs. Our fantasies were also fueled by the mountain of costumes in the shed on the back edge of a neighbor's lot. As if from Heaven, a refrigerator box chock full of clowns suits, pirate gear, tutus, hats and glittery fabric sat waiting for a kids' endless imagination.

One day I was in there alone trying out some new combinations when through the back boards I saw a man in a long sleeved red shirt run nearby. Later at home, I heard on the radio that a prisoner had escaped and we were to keep an eye out for a man in a long sleeved red shirt. He had such fear on his face when he passed the shed that I felt bad for him so I decided not to say anything.

Several neighbors became my Grandparents as the last of my own had died when I was four. Considering friends and neighbors as family become a natural feeling as more of mine disappeared. Anyway, with all those grandparents Halloween was HUGE! Our bags were always loaded with the usual mini chocolates, peanut butter cups, candy corn and that perfunctory apple, but one eagerly awaited treat was the giant cookie 'special baked' by Minnie Marvin. She'd drop it in our bag unwrapped so by the time we got home it was just big crumbles, but the best crumbles you could imagine.

Minnie Marvin was happy, happy, happy. She was maybe five feet tall, grandma plump and wore absolutely huge shorts. Her hair was a white woman Afro with about seventeen grey strands per square inch. Everything about her house was busy. Busy and happy. The upholstery was in various patterns of flowered bark cloth, shelves of knick knacks were everywhere and the pink living room walls framed endless family pictures. She was always baking, the aromas lending to the aura of a real life gingerbread house. She even had a parakeet named 'Happy' although I doubt that was the case, a bird caged all its life. None the less, he chirped all day and Minnie paid quite a bit of attention to him.

During my visits I would sit on the floor by the sofa hugging the life sized ceramic statue of a Lassie dog and play with all the jewelry around its neck. She'd go about wrapping goody packages, checking her violets and scratching Happy's head, humming a lively tune and never seeming to mind answering the stream of questions I would throw at her. Her grandchildren must have adored her. I know I did.

SECTION TWO

DONNA REED and FATHER KNOWS BEST on TV
DONA STEINLE and MOTHER KNOWS BEST
in REAL LIFE

SPRING CLEANING

I'm not exactly sure when we sold the big house across the street that Dad built, the one in front of the old barn, but considering our financial status it was probably after Red and Pat Robertson had left their mark. I was still little, but not so young that Red's 'crime boss' demeanor escaped me. He wore his jet black hair in a greased up pompadour and a black suit dressed up his businessman's body of barrel chest and big belly. While his thick rubbery lips were often smiling, a fat cigar rolled back and forth between them. I didn't know it then but his smell was alcohol and smoke covered heavily by aftershave. His eyes were glaring and snake like.

Pat was pretty and curvy with ever changing hair color and a fake baby coo laugh that was authentic not that many years back. It was about her that I first heard the word 'Ditzy'. On one occasion she decided that some serious cleaning was in order and figured out all by herself that the most efficient way to get the job done would be to drag in the garden hose and tackle it all in one washing. She went through every room. After that some very different words were used to describe her.

The once lovely house my father had built was no more. The electrical system became problematic. Various ceilings drooped and dropped in places, mold spores gathered for their continual raids, paint peeled and the Linoleum buckled in every room. But the roof, cement walls and floor all stood soundly and by the time I was aware it was owned by someone else. The absentee landlord had fixed nothing but the rent was cheap and there were a lot of rooms for too many kids so it attracted large poor families. While the neighborhood was not originally designed for rentals, only one family ever posed a problem after the Robertson's bolted.

NOT EXACTLY HASBRO

The best part of that property from a kid's stand point was that big old barn out back. Mother never entered the place and the neighbors had no interest whatsoever in what went on in there. It was two stories high with only a partial second floor for parking tall machinery. Even so, there were several rooms with a big floor in front of them. There was no railing so it was perfect for staging plays and mock 'Fights of the Old West'. We'd dress up in all the old discarded clothes and feign death, falling on to the mountain of filthy mattresses we pulled from the rooms and piled down below.

The ground floor was open except for two small rooms. Exploded home canning jars lined the shelves of the 'kitchen' with knives and other utensils scattered near the big rusty sink. A kid could lie flat out on the counter next to it to play the part of 'Experiment #6' as that room had been deemed a mad scientists laboratory.

The remains of a bathroom opened to the right of the 'laboratory' housing one seriously foul toilet. Next to it was a tiny sink, its own putrid goo captured mirror shards that had dropped from the frame above, others littered the floor. A cracked glass shelf displayed rusty razor blades. The metal shower stall was covered in dark blotches of fuzz and a mound of stiffened towel like substance rose from the floor. None of us used 'the facilities' but a few of the boys occasionally peed on the cloth to see if it would grow.

The large open area offered all sorts of tools and machinery, many sharply pronged, and the parts that flattened or pinched were still movable. Good stuff for recreating scenes from our favorite Saturday morning cartoons. An old refrigerator and gas stove stood at the ready to suffocate or explode and the rusting gas cans weren't empty. A long heavy chain hung from the ceiling which made a fantastic swing that most of us could easily straddle or drape over the big hook at the end.

It was a perfect playground for barefoot country kids who were simply let loose to play until suppertime.

UNNECESSARY WALLS

That big house that Dad built was the only one like it in the neighborhood. Most of the others were one story ranches with carports, the original and more varied versions of todays cranked out rectangles. Mother told me that when they first arrived, an acre of land in that area was going for a nickel. I guess my Dad had a few dimes to spare. The house he built for us was also a one off. The living room was huge as was the kitchen and there was only a partial wall in between them. Both my parents were from Brooklyn so I came to think that the women there didn't like being shut away when cooking and when I bought my house the first thing I did was to knock down a similar dividing wall. The third house he got to build was the newer version ranch he was hired and that's what the new landlord insisted on.

As I said my Dad died from an aneurysm. I was about five when it was explained to me that a blood vessel popped in his brain and flooded it. A clear visual of that formed in my own brain and that's how I described it when asked. My Mother was taken to task about the impropriety of being so graphic with a young child.

When I first came to the town I now call home, I met a couple with a toddler and was introduced to her cat who she'd named Clitoris. Hilarious and yes, a little awkward for certain people, but what harm was done? The kid had apparently asked about one of her own body parts, was truthfully told and she thought the word was pretty. These people are still my friends, their daughter is a happy, well-adjusted, highly successful person and my own particular early education fostered a keen interest in the inner workings of the body.

ANN and ARTHUR

My neighborhood was teaming with the offerings of colorful people to glean from and Mother encouraged visiting as long as we were welcome.

The school bus dropped us off in front of Ann Zellafrow's house and since she had two daughters an open invitation was extended. Being in the middle of Terry and Kathy's wide age gap, I connected with both.

My Mother was older than most with school aged children and Parkinson's disease had her since I could remember but she still looked like a Mom. Thinking of the woman I was introduced to that first day as a Mom seemed as unlikely as that mink heiress thing.

There's an episode of 'Seinfeld' showing a neighbor of Kramers' in that famous Gloria Swanson role. It was a facsimile of that neighbor I was being led toward but without the sit-com humor to soften the experience. She was 'Ready for her Close Up, Mr. DeMille' and would be so every time I saw her. Holding out a gnarling claw with long red fingernails she smiled out the lowest, slowest "How do you do?" I'd ever heard from a female. Smeared lipstick matched the nail color accenting tawny teeth.

Undoubtedly beautiful before her troubles, she was still looking through that distant mirror. Long black hair and heavy evening makeup accentuated her eyes, her skin dusty from over powdering, the beauty mark an obvious fake. Fur covered pillows surrounded her as she sat in photo pose on a gold velvet sofa with lions paws carved in the wooden arms and feet. A sparkly black dress, low cut and split up the side revealed too much body for a Wednesday afternoon visit from a child. Her feet were bare, the stilettos rejecting the twisted toes.

The air was thick with perfume and body odor blessedly tempered by the year round open windows. Her life was displayed on the coffee table in front of her. Hollywood magazines and countless empty Coca-Cola bottles lay drained and tired like the woman who guzzled them. Smoke from a volcanic ashtray of Viceroy butts snaked around the one burning in her hand. A caché of pills begged from a nearby bowl. The TV blared out an old black and white movie.

Standing in front of her, mouth agape and trying to figure out "How I did", she started in on the tale I would hear every visit thereafter. And there were many, as the initial bizarreness turned to fascination and then adoration from a newly devoted fan.

Apparently, she and Arthur Godfrey were secret lovers and had been so since the early 40's. She was a brilliant actress and reminded me at every telling. Arthur looked for unknown talent for his radio shows in small theater productions and came across one of her performances. Within minutes he was enamored with not only her abilities but with her, and soon after their meeting, she with him.

Arthur Godfrey was an entertainment pioneer for decades, gaining his first radio experience in the Navy. His free thinking Dad was strong willed, openly opinionated and directly influential. Unlike other announcers' stiff, impersonal manner of talking at people, he took a conversational approach and an adoring audience was born. He secured the endearment of his fans with his sly sense of humor, like pronouncing Bayer Aspirin, one of the shows sponsors, BareAss Prin. During a show in South Florida he proclaimed they were in Miami Bitch, chuckling afterward throughout the airwaves. This was provocative stuff in those days.

In the late '40's he headed up a popular TV show called 'Arthur Godfrey's Talent Show' which helped the careers of several still highly revered entertainers such as Patsy Cline, Pat Boone and Tony Bennett.

Here's where Ann's story takes hold. They were together for around five years prior to that particular show's beginning, blissful yet hidden, as he was married at the time. She vowed he'd gotten the idea for the new show to showcase her enormous talent without suspicion of any 'undercover' activities. She would always wink a massive eyelash at this point.

In the early 1950's Ann began to experience chronic and severe pain in her joints, mainly one hip. Arthur had been in a serious automobile accident in 1931 that left him with reoccurring pain as well. He had heard about a controversial procedure that he alone decided was the answer to both their physical problems, so in 1953 they each underwent hip replacement surgery. I can't begin to imagine what that entailed at that time but it couldn't have been the snap, crackle, pop it in place procedure routinely done today. His good fortune was a complete success much to the relief of his friends and fans. Her ill fate was a complete failure and shared with no one behind lonely doors kept closed by many a greased palm. Not only was her pain intensified but the replacement was not a proper fit, making her somewhat lopsided.

This presented innumerable complications and as I dissected this story, it seemed that keeping the secrecy of the whole situation was the most important problem to Arthur. It was commonplace knowledge that Arthur's 'on air' persona did not portray every strand in his pot of emotional spaghetti. In fact, behind the scenes he could be quite the tyrant. He'd been quoted as once warning his staff, "Remember, many of you are here over the bodies I have personally slain. I've done it before and I can do it again." Ann may have been one of those bodies.

According to Ann though, Arthur was devastated by her results. His prize talent discovery and only real true love was in dire straits. He bought her a house in Florida, having more suitable recovery weather and set out to retain the finest doctor the world had to offer to not only replace the defective hip but provide the cure for her crippling arthritis. A movie was in the works specifically written for her talents to shine as bright as the Heavens and filming would begin the minute she was able bodied.

Now I don't know what is true or not here, but I do know that my neighbor sat on a prop couch in a retirement village every day for years in full actress garb, drugged out of her mind to ease the pain of a faulty hip replacement, waiting for Arthur Godfrey to walk through the door and make her a star.

MEETING AUNT POO-POO HEAD

Living next door to this unbalanced tragedy was an elderly couple appropriately named the Witts. Both were retired college professors in their nineties, over six feet tall and spoke words of sentence length in my young presence. They were a favorite visit but I experienced a mild unreasoned fear at first meeting and then again a few years later. My armchair psychiatry came up with possible causes...

I met my maternal grandfather for the first and only time when I was four years old. We took the train from Dade City to Queens to visit my Mother's sister Ruth's family and their live-in father, a long retired NYC horse cop. Eight year old Bob burst with responsibility pride as he was allowed to ride and sleep alone in an upright seat while Mother and I shared a Pullman car. The continuous mild motion gave me the best sleep I have ever had. Have bed manufacturers given a thought to the rocking cradle option?

Being inside Grand Central Station panicked me to no end. The place was huge and packed with people, many of whom were running and smacking their hard alligator suitcases into various parts of my body, me being the proper receiving height and of a lesser concern. The ceiling was dizzyingly high, silver and domed like a spaceship. Everything was crowded and fast, the opposite of my life up to that point.

I have no memory of what must have been the pure madness of a cab ride to their apartment building. Screaming was my general reaction to most discomforting situations and when the little room we had just entered began moving I reacted in kind. Heading to the 600th floor, the first 572 levels did not escape my lung power. I was reduced to sobbing out my fear by the time giant Aunt Ruth greeted us but that caused a harsh look of disdain to cross her face which unnerved me even more.

Once inside the apartment I was sent to their all white living room, ordered not to touch anything and ignored. My Grandfather soon entered. His own giantness caused him to duck his head under the doorjamb and the pajamas he wore were very loose and rather revealing. I had never seen any man like that, in pajamas or otherwise, never mind that tall. The white room was ghostlike and my aunt's mean looks had me jittery. He gruffed out a 'Hello' almost in my direction and fear overtook. I bellowed like a coyote and dove behind the sofa where I stayed for hours. No one tried to comfort me and that's the last I saw of my Grandfather.

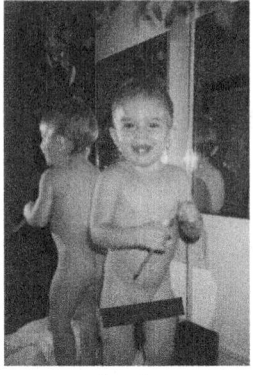 

Stephan   *Bob and me as toddlers*
A Mother's humor!

In our room that night, Mother apologized to me and said she was just honoring the house rules. I could stay in the room as long as I liked, which I gladly did unless escorted by Mother.

Aunt Ruth had some kind of hold over my Mother. I didn't like her and somewhere along the line I started calling her Aunt Poo-Poo Head which my Mother never corrected.

THE SUCKING STAIRS

The Witts were even taller and older than my Grandfather and at first reminded me of that awful trip. However they proved to be engaging, welcoming people who were always happy to see me so that initial fear quickly subsided. I would sit on the floor in their small living room made smaller by the floor to ceiling bookshelves and eat the saucer sized chocolate chip cookies Mrs. Witt had freshly baked. It was usually Mr. Witt who would lounge in his chair and talk about things I knew nothing about, perfect for a little sponge. Sometimes he would open up his shop in the garage and show me how to bring the beauty out of rough stones, then how to turn them into jewelry pieces. He educated me about garden tools and pointed out the differences in plant leaves. He brought me along into whatever he felt like doing. He tended beautiful rose bushes and I was often sent home with a generous bouquet of flowers for Mother. My favorite bracelet was from him and we even built a bird feeder together.

On one visit, I found him sitting in his back yard with a shot gun blasting blue jays away from that feeder. It wildly upset me until he explained that he was just 'spraying' them enough to scare them off. That's what I was told anyway and I chose to believe it.

The second onset of fear of these lovely people came from a cartoon. My brother was given some Playboys early on and he let me read them. A comedian by nature, I always gravitated to magazines with lots of jokes in them. Reader's Digest was a good one for that and Mother would let me wait in the longest line of the grocery store to read "Laughter, the Best Medicine" and hopefully have time for "Humor in Uniform".

In Playboy, there was (is?) a full page color cartoon every month by the cartoonist Gahan Wilson. Many of his characters were drawn with wrinkled outlines which evoked a shakiness and were made to look ancient no matter what age they represented. They had big, sad eyes with loose skin around them, giving the frightening appearance of not being able to hold the eyeball in much longer. The smiles showed most of the teeth in a skeletal referral. The hands were large, the fingers long and bony.

One cartoon showed a 'Down' escalator full of people. The front couple was getting sucked under the bottom plate that covered the moving steps. (We've all had that thought, right?) Well, that couple looked exactly like the Witts! I was shocked and wary at first, wondering if they were even alive but soon realized the humor. I also developed a slight bond of an unknown nature with Mr. Gahan Wilson.

DRIVING LESSONS

The Witts and the Zellefrows lived on Bailey Hill Rd, the one road in our 'hood' that continued over the hill and back down through the orange groves. Another of our play spots was right next to the railroad tracks at the bottom of that hill. It was a massive clay ditch we named the Little Grand Canyon, maybe 12 feet wide and deep, the end going around a forbidden (to us) curve. The Florida heat would often dry out the surface leaving formidable clay chips that would explode into a fine rusty powder after a womp on someone's head. Deep crevices lined the sides large enough for a kid to hide in and one went up right under the train tracks, leaving one rail just hanging in the air for an ever lengthening distance. The desert like conditions inspired us to play 'Old West' and we couldn't wait until the day the train would get hung up and plummet into the canyon, just like in the movies!

Bob taught me how to drive on Bailey Hill, in the orange groves and on nearby Fort King Rd. which went directly over La Houp Hill, one of the highest points in Florida. He was also only learning and Mother believed we stayed in the orange groves as directed. He did practice his donuts there but we included going too fast down the bumpy side of Baily Hill in order to lift the old Ford off the ground and once just after cresting the top of La Houp, he put his foot over mine on the gas pedal. My Bejeezus was hot with fear as I frantically tried to keep the wheels straight to stay on the asphalt. Regular driving was simple after these lessons. For the record, I was eight, Bob twelve.

EDNA'S MEAT DISCS

The other end of Bailey Hill teed into the southbound lanes of Highway 301, which was considered the front of our neighborhood. On the corner was a little restaurant called the Valley View, named for the gorgeous pastoral scene across the road. It kind of resembled the White House. The middle section bowed out so cars could nose up for curb service or you could walk up to one of several windows to order ice cream cones and other heat beating treats. There were uneven wings on either side for indoor seating, originally built for 'white' and 'colored', the kitchen was in the center back, accessing while separating both sides.

These roadside diners were privately owned and radiated the distinct personality drawn from their owners. The 'Freezette' for example, on Dade City's south end, had a picnic like feel to it, with its screened porch and communal tables. An active community minded couple owned it and you could feel that they put their hearts and souls into the place. It was lively and bustling from lunch til midnight, attracting families, groups of rowdy teens, and daters simultaneously. Smiling waitresses and often the owners themselves would serve baskets of golden fried grouper, thick juicy burgers and sumptuous milk shakes, while the juke box kept the chatter level on the raucous side. It was a real occasion for us to eat there and we went as often as we could afford, which as it happened wasn't very.

The Valley View was the exact opposite. This 3 dimensional definition of the word 'dreary' was owned by one Edna Hoster. She and her daughter Ruth lived in the smaller wing, big enough for two twin beds and a chest of drawers. A small portable TV sat on top in front of a mocking mirror and a tiny bathroom cowered behind the back wall. The cement block was originally painted a prison green color but had paled to an even sadder hue.

The other wing was the dining room. The tables, never having been pushed together for a large party, had found secure footing in the greasy dirt surrounding each leg. The picture windows were covered by shabby yellowed curtains, allowing only a film of the famous Florida sun in and blocking out the beautiful sweeping expanse of the restaurant's namesake. The back wall held the only other window, tiny and set into a door leading to the spider ridden outdoor toilet, lit by a hanging bare bulb. It took exactly one visit for me to steer clear and learn to 'hold it' until we got home. The large blank wall opposite the kitchen carried three dime store prints far too small for the space only emphasizing the grimness. The ice cream porch was closed.

An industrial shelf unit carried the obligatory conch shell lamps and landscapes made from the seashells the state regularly coughed up. Plastic palms, orange trees, gators and flamingoes stood on glued down beach sand and fronds. Once everywhere, they're now considered 'vintage', collectors seeking out the more intricate ones.

Mother took us there for Sunday dinner at least once a month and occasionally for a midweek meal. Mother did not like to cook, partially because of her Parkinson's disease and partly because she didn't like to cook. She did make homemade spaghetti sauce once in a while and that was one happy day. A big open pot would simmer on the stove top all afternoon filling the house with the rich scent of oregano and she'd let me have a spoonful every so often as her official taste tester. At the table I could use the big green Jell-O bowl and would fill it three times before I was done. We all ate heartily on spaghetti night.

Mother felt duty bound to contribute her share to the struggling women as she too felt the strain from lack of income left by an absent partner. So off we'd go. Bob found ways to get out of it, but I didn't mind. I was a sturdy little Hoover of a kid that would eat anything set in front of me and to either side.

What was served was expected from a place bestowed with such a tragic personality. It was edible though, considering it was well before America's reawakening to fresh food. The weekday meal consisted of some sort of breaded meat disc covered in a tan gelatinous substance including a deep fried fish square for those Friday people. A gluey plop of tan, canned peas, mushy creamed corn or lard laden greens accompanied said disc. I usually went for the hot dogs. It was all about the ice cream anyway. Sunday dinner was special and there would be at least one other table eating whenever we showed up. Fried chicken and real mashed potatoes along with a pale green lettuce and tomato salad. AND a sliver of cake came with that ice cream.

During the week, Mother and I ate alone and Edna or Ruth would come out to chat with us. I use the term 'chat' loosely when Edna would appear. She'd stand at the table, arms crossed, sneering at the air and complain about nothing and everything. Her expression was permanently bound in irritated disappointment which over time had carved the spider web of wrinkles that covered her face. Her bone structure told of an attractive woman but the thick layer of anger and resentment made catching even a glimpse of beauty a monumental task. Her teeth were long gone, but since she rarely smiled you'd never notice unless she was as much a part of your life as she was of mine. The threadbare uniform, baggy sweater and rolled down support hose looked purposefully done to present poorly.

Once when I ran over to borrow some morning milk, I saw her hair undone and flowing gracefully down her back in a lovely wave. Her cotton nightgown gave clues to the shapely figure she still owned but refused to acknowledge. She even smiled when she gave me the bottle. The next time we ate there and that snarling mouth started yapping, I tried, really tried to picture that softer version but it got all discombobulated. I also noticed my Mother's jaw steeled when attempting to add some brightness to the 'conversation'. Edna Hoster was no easy peach to digest.

Oh, but I loved Ruth! The whole room lit up when she was in it. Always an ear to ear smile and sparkly brown eyes full of life and love. Her skin was rough and her dark hair was just like 'Nancy' in the funny papers. She was curvaceous too but the left side of her body sagged, the foot dragged and the hand fell limp. Her laugh was often and real. A gold necklace and matching earrings with blue stones complimented her crisp blue form fitting uniform. She'd always have a special little shell or something for me and our eyes danced with sheer joy as she put it in my hand. She was beautiful.

When I found out that she was the one who made all the lamps and landscapes I was dumbfounded. It never occurred to me that someone had created those things, let alone by my Ruth. They were just there...everywhere. She would sit with us and we'd all get to giggling, my Mother's jaw comfortable in movement. Sometimes Edna would join us and stand over Ruth, spewing out sour comments through her fixed grimace. She kept her hands on the back of the chair, never a loving touch for her daughter as my Mother so naturally did. But Ruth kept smiling, making our dinner palatable. What a magical woman!

Edna had a nephew named Gregory who visited from time to time from I don't know where. He would arrive after flying down Greer Hill on his bicycle. His body clearly stated that he lived on that bike. I loved his visits. He was comfortable with us as a group but paid attention to each one of our interests. He never ate anything but the ice cream. Hah! Pretty AND smart.

One day Edna told us that Gregory wasn't able to visit that afternoon as planned. Her demeanor was noticeably devoid of complaint or annoyance. He'd been racing down the hill as usual when a car crossed in front of him. He and his bike slid under it, the back wheel running over his chest. "You could see the tire tracks go right across his t-shirt!" she beamed, unmistakably proud. As it turned out, the car was tiny and he was so strong and muscular that it didn't kill him, barely even hurt him in fact. Edna Hoster was heard humming a song for the next few days. It took a lot of doing for a person to make that woman happy.

BUILDING A RELATIONSHIP

A personal grove of orange trees stood between the restaurant and the house of the human Tweety Bird, a small bald Swedish man with huge blue eyes and pursed lips which transformed into a warm wide smile. I'm not sure I ever got his name right, but I loved visiting as he was always in his backyard shop building whirly-gigs, those wind powered yard decorations with the moving parts. Two men sawing a log. A boy peddling a bicycle with a dog running behind wagging his tail. A woman cooling a pie by waving a towel over it. A real piece of cloth that the wind blew! I found them fascinating. His yard displayed several complex models, but he made hundreds of simpler versions over the years which disappeared soon after they were given life. My visits were mainly to catch sight of them before they were shipped off to some tourist shop to sit alongside the shell lamps, alligator coin purses and key chains dangling the 'lucky' rabbit's foot, dyed in brilliant colors perhaps to disguise the truth a bit. I think Ruth and he worked together. He did seem to be quite happy in his retirement.

MY FIRST SERIAL KILLER

Our school bus changed routes in fourth grade making our new drop off point across the highway in front of the gift shop. The really weird gift shop. Waiting out the rain was my only reason for ever going in. It was dark, dusty and crammed full of touristy stuff although I never once saw a customer. A mother and son lived in the back half of the tiny building. The woman never smiled and the boy would stand in the doorway staring at me with vacant, yet evil eyes. He gave me the creeps and I stayed away from him.

One week night we went to dinner at the Valley View and to my surprise several of the neighbors were also there. We ordered and when I became engrossed with my food Mother went over and joined them. I pretended not to listen but how else was I going to find out what was up? Apparently a tortured and mercifully now dead cat had been found in the field and everyone was agreeing that the boy from the gift shop did it. My skin crawled. I would later read that serial killers had often been animal torturers as children, but what I had heard just then was enough for me to wait in the rain for the bus. They moved away much to everyone's relief and possible insistence and the shop remained closed as long as we lived there.

BONGOS AND COWBOYS

That fear and the fact that the bus consistently dropped us off a few minutes past the start of my favorite cartoon, The Flintstones, turned me into one of the fastest runners in the sixth grade. I would leap off the bus and at top speed race to the house, in through the kitchen, right hand extended to grab the bag of Pecan Sandies on the counter and slide into home in front of the TV, praying I hadn't missed too much. The Gleason inference was over my head but I so loved the appliances, the elephant shower, the sarcastic pterodactyl duster, the bird beak record player, the dinosaur stairs, the ticket punching Rhino. Hilarious!

Anyway, all that running combined with my normally active playtime kept my weight somewhat under control considering my Pop-Tart intake. At least the muscles underneath that fat were toned. I won races, even beating out the boys a few times. My method was to run a good steady pace the first three quarters, and then imagine having the spinning legs of a fleeing cartoon character, even hearing the bongos, and fly past everyone else. Isn't it amazing what the mind can make the body do?

Not particularly sports minded, there were no scheduled practices to enhance my ability. My 'fitness routine' in those days was just your basic cause and effect of daily life. Bob had offered a lawn mowing service to the neighborhood and many of them gladly paid the $4.00 fee to get their two and a half acres mowed. He would do one every afternoon, two in the heavy growing season. Not bad money for a preteen back then and it kept him in good shape as well. We had a small but heavy electric mower with a long cord and an extension for the back fields. As he got older and acquired more of a social life, I began to fill in for him and eventually took the whole business over. Figuring out how to mow around the trees without tangling the cord only took one mow and whipping it over the shorter bushes became a game. Like my friend Mickey says, "Work is Fun'.

You Have Now Entered....THE TWILIGHT ZONE

The commissioned house my Dad had built next door was first occupied by a retired couple named Dwyer. They moved out when my brain still had no limits and the only other time I saw them was in a comic strip. Looking through the funnies as I loved to do, I came across a strip about a brother and sister living in Orlando. The brother looked just like Mr. Dwyer and for a short while before I was corrected, I thought that's where they had moved. Coincidentally in my twenties, Lynn (from the Mennonite group home days 'After' described in a later chapter) finally succeeded in reconnecting with me. She told me that in her search she had reached a retiree named Bob Steinle, whose sister Anne had recently died. They had been living together in Orlando! Kind of Twilight Zonish, don't you think? And I now live where Rod Serling wrote and filmed many of those shows. Do-do-do-do...

Speaking of the Twilight Zone, who remembers the episode with the little boy who was getting weaker with each passing day and no one could figure out the cause? In the last scene the worried

Mother tucks him in and leaves the door slightly open as she says good night. In the light beam and assured that the Mother is gone, the eyes of the boy's teddy bear pop open and a malicious grin reveals a set of sharp fangs. Not only was that ending a jump starter to the heart, but my poor brother had a teddy bear that looked exactly like the evil one. Aaaauuuggghhh!!! He ran to his room, grabbed it, flew down the hall and threw it in the vacuum cleaner closet. Mother made sure he never saw it again.

Mr. Serlings' shows taught us lessons that went deeper than the standard 'good guy wins' that other shows presented. How should you react when too many appliances break down? If I recall, the man finally threw himself out the kitchen window. I believe the lesson there was that this might be an 'over' reaction. What is considered beautiful is only opinion, as with the plastic surgery episode. Never seeing any faces until the last minute, the patient emerges from her unsuccessful surgery as a beautiful woman of modern America and everyone else, shocked and revolted by her ugliness, sports a huge forehead, twisted froggish mouth and nose holes. (Kind of like a kid in my third grade class if truth be told.) From the classic library episode with Bertrand Russell, I picked up two things...life just plain sucks sometimes and don't waste time in a bad relationship.

While you're off remembering your own favorite episodes, I'll get back to my 'hood'.

The Dwyer house sat empty for a while and some of the kids and I put on a play for the neighborhood in the carport. I wrote it; something about a Queen which I played of course and little Terry was my court jester. One of my lines to her was, "You're very funny, aren't you?" She was wearing my brother's Halloween clown costume and replied perfectly "Yes I am, amn't I?" Everyone laughed out loud and again I must praise the neighborhood grandparents we kids were blessed with.

Terry had huge blonde curls, blue eyes and a gorgeous smile. She had the bone structure of a tall woman and her skin was a beautiful caramel color. It later became obvious to me that she and Ruth both had black fathers and I've wondered from time to time just who did the shunning. Terry would have been a stunning woman had a hit and run driver not killed her. I never saw Ann or Kathy after that as they moved away, but was eventually told that Terry was Kathy's daughter, not Ann's. My heart still goes out to both of those poor women.

MY CRIMINAL PAST

The Cooke family was next in the Dwyer house after that nightmare and they stayed until we moved into town. There was a mother, a boy, three girls and a father who drove a truck and was gone during the week. Every weekend there was a box for us that had 'fallen of the truck'. When he delivered Sara Lee products the German chocolate cake period was a big favorite. One night the kids came over for spaghetti dinner and the brother showed us how to get our tongues stuck in a coke bottle. Well, stuck they got! Coke bottles can get heavy when it's only your tongue carrying the weight, but we still couldn't stop laughing.

The oldest was Kathy and three years my senior. She and Bob spent a good bit of time together. She once confessed to me that after fooling around out in the woods, he took her clothes and drove her through town naked in his open truck bed. She seemed to have enjoyed the experience, but something about it made my stomach churn.

Kathy introduced me to her criminal mind and decided we needed to see how our breaking and entering skills measured up by using some of the out of town neighbor's houses as practice. A younger sister included, we picked two houses that were empty on the same night and had discussions on how to do it 'properly'. Our clothes were all black and one of us even had a ski mask. Taping over the back door window, we quietly tapped it with a cloth wrapped hammer until the glass was cracked and lifted out in one piece. A gloved hand reached in and unlocked the door. A tiny flash light pointed to the floor was our only light and using a pillowcase, we gathered all sorts of silver things. We got out fast and hid the sack under a weeping bush in the victims own back yard. We had no interest in the goods; it was the execution of the crime.

On to the other house and we were done. We had to slice the screen along the back corner of the porch to get in, but other than that, it was the same routine. This time we took a few pieces of jewelry, one was a gold ring with a red stone and we buried them out by the utility shed.

This was done on a Friday night and the next night Mother called me home from an overnight stay at a friends' house. A police car was in the driveway. Uh-Oh! The officer was talking with my Mother as I walked in. "May I ask you a few questions?" he yawned and without pausing informed me that there had been a few robberies the night before and could I offer anything of help? I acted completely surprised and said I knew nothing. When he said…and I quote… "Well, this was obviously done by professionals" I almost said "Thank you" and caught my smile just in time. I never heard any more about it except that the first hit finally found their stuff under that bush and the widow in the other house who always seemed a bit nervous was now a lot more nervous. I don't waste much time on regrets, but this one's a biggie.

Another sensible choice of entertainment had Kathy and me skipping school and taking a bus to Tampa. It turned out that we were the only females on this bus and also the only white people. Everyone had on jeans, white t-shirts, and the same kind of shoes (government issue I would later learn). I assumed at the time that they were a singing group or belonged to some club. (The 'club' was prison and they were out on day release.) Kathy seemed to be a little jumpy at first after realizing we had gotten on (and allowed on) the wrong bus, but when one of the guys asked me where we were headed, I started babbling away as usual and we ended up having a grand old time telling funny stories and we all waved back and forth as we departed.

Kathy wanted to go to the big Maas Brothers department store in south Tampa. We had no money, but she soon came over, opened her hand and excitedly whispered in my ear "Look what I have!" She had stolen a piece of jewelry and urged me to do the same. I went over to a glass case and there was a string of beads curled up on the counter. Cupped it up like a pro and stuck it in my pocket. We wandered a while longer, our crimes quickly forgotten. As we were leaving the store, a woman came running toward us. It was that same woman who was standing next to me at the jewelry counter. I politely held the door open for her and she grabbed us by the collars and hauled our thieving little butts upstairs to the in-store police annex.

Detective Flo Jones, I will never forget you! She didn't believe either one of us when we told her our ages of 12 and 15 which put us under prosecution age, but our parents confirmed it over the phone while agreeing that yes, we were too big for our britches. We were put into official steel barred lockdown to wait the hour it took our parents to arrive. It seemed much longer. They drove separately so thankfully I didn't have to deal with Kathy's father. She told me he was furious and hollered his sage advice of, "If you're going to steal, don't get caught!"

Mother took a different approach. After the releasing process and a few miles down the road she finally broke the deafening silence by quietly stating, "I'm very disappointed in you". WHOA! I could feel my chest cave in and my heart fall into the hole it created. Disappointing someone you love is physically painful. I do NOT recommend it. My crime spree was over.

SIX FEET OF ???

The day I finally met the father in person was a Saturday morning while talking with Mrs. Cooke as she was making breakfast. She was short and round with tight little pin curly hair, cat eye glasses and I thought her to be in her late forties like Mother. I mean no offense here but she reminded me of a bulldog. Her chin stuck out prominently and when she smiled you could see most of her teeth. Her fat little cheeks were high and made her eyes squint. She was generous and caring, although she did tend to yell a lot.

All of a sudden six feet of sex eased into the room, snuck up behind her and squeezed her barely covered nipples. I hadn't noticed what she was wearing before but now I could see completely through her sheer nightgown. She slapped his hands away, barked "Not in front of the children!" and went back to flipping the bacon. He leisurely slid his hands along her shoulders to massage her neck and winked at me along with a soft throaty chuckle.

I stood frozen in place. Mouth agape and of their own control my eyes widened to take in this new picture. My brain was telling me that this was a loving husband and father of four but every other part of me saw nothing but that six feet of sex thing. His form fitting jeans and tight white t-shirt only emphasized his muscular thighs and forearms. His entire body seemed to be in a slight constant motion, swaying back and forth like the sea, holding back a wave that was craving to reach your shore and wash over every part of you. My eyes were all over him but kept going back to that forearm, muscles rippling as he rubbed his wife's neck. (Oh right, there was someone else in the room.) And those perfect thighs, slightly rocking to some quiet music only their owner could hear.

I dared to look up at his face and fell right into his deep brown eyes, his luscious mouth grinning with joy at my indulgence, but I was too engrossed to be embarrassed. I was drinking in something fresh and delicious and wanted to learn the ingredients. Here was an example of a perfect recipe and I felt compelled to study it. But what was compelling me?

Continuing my research, my mind wandered to them as a pair. Could this really be her husband? He looked to be about 28, passionately out of control like a wild stallion. She looked and acted organized and matronly. He did come home every weekend and seemed to be quite attracted to her. He was certainly Kathy's dad as she had his distinct upper lip and burning brown eyes. Why the puzzle? I'd heard a couple starts to look alike in later years and I was surrounded by couples in their later years. All my Mother's friends were closely matched in age and several did have a similar appearance. Apparently, I took that to be the way it was. These two were different in every way possible. Yes in age and looks, but also in behavior and style. Yet here they were, happy and compatible in a cramped little house with four kids and not much else. Okay then.

Six Feet of Sex left early Monday mornings, muffling his big rig for the neighbors benefit. Mrs. Cooke went into town one afternoon and left us on our own for several hours. We decided to check out their bedroom. (I swear, I never did this kind of stuff with anyone else but this family). One helped another up and we found a pile of paperbacks on the top shelf in their closet. Book club commenced.

Holy Moly! These were the nastiest books I'd ever seen and I had leafed through more than one Playboy. These were story books though, if you could call them that, no pictures. We all chose a comfy spot and got into some serious reading. Every once in a while one of us would gasp or chuckle, but for five kids left alone all afternoon we were exceedingly quiet. These books got me thinking that maybe this was one of the bonds Mr. and Mrs. Cooke had with each other. The 'behind closed doors' stuff I'd only heard about. Yikes! Is this part of sex? It all sounded so painful and degrading. Six Feet of Sex or not, no thank you!

COOKIES and SEX

The two rental houses were the only ones that brought in younger parents, but that didn't mean there was no other sex happening in the neighborhood. Kitty-cornered to our house lived a content couple named the Rogers. Their entire property was covered with as many trees, lush plants and flowers as they could possibly pack in. Only pathways and sitting areas were in back, one spot holding an often used hammock. (I'm presently heading that way with my yard.) A clear view of their backyard goings on could be seen from my Mulberry tree, although there was no need to spy as I visited a lot. See, they had a lamp in their living room with a shade that came alive and I was mesmerized by it. When lit, the waterfall flowed and the trees fluttered their leaves. It was right by the front door and I was allowed to walk in, sit on the sofa and switch the light on and off for The Show. Mrs. Rogers might be in the kitchen baking some delicious sweetness with the whistling Mr. puttering in the yard. It was a comfortable situation.

One afternoon the need for The Show arose and did I ever get one. As I entered, my eyes immediately followed left toward the muffled grunts and giggles my ears were hearing. Their bedroom door was open and I could see two sets of bare legs flailing about on their bed. I may have been too young to know the finer details, but I did know the basics and quickly skedaddled leaving them to finish what I did not care to witness. They didn't hear me so there was no awkwardness, but I did start knocking first and waited until one of them answered before I came in.

NO SEX HERE

A different kind of sexual encounter occurred, not so innocent but fortunately having no lasting negative effect. Mother and I had walked up to visit some neighbors one day, Romeo and Sylvia. Despite his namesake, Romeo seemed drained of most of his life forces. His skin and muscles hung from his bones, even on his face. He had huge ears and his smile was upside down. His hands shook much worse than Mother's and made everything else about him seem unsteady.

Sylvia was in perfect health except for her missing teeth. Her constant yard work and Italian background resulted in clear dark skin and brimming with energy she kept the house gleaming despite the low light. During one of our special visits while we snacked on salted raw onions over the kitchen counter, she confessed that she stood in that same place to eat her dinner while her husband sat at the table. I remember the loneliness in that is what struck me.

On this visit she guided us through their immaculate house and shyly bragged over some embroidered handkerchiefs in the hall closet she had recently done. As we walked back through the narrow hallway with me trailing, the bathroom door opened and Romeo stopped me. Mumbling in a whisper, his trembling hands cupped my face. He stumbled as he leaned in to press his lips on mine, stinky tobacco juice running down my chin. He grabbed one of his wife's prized linens and wiped my mouth, patted my bottom and sent me on my way. I was mad at him for ruining his wife's needlework and disgusted by the tobacco juice. I would learn the word 'pathetic' later and connect it to this incident. Entering the kitchen, Mother surprised me by quickly saying our good-byes and steering me out the door.

We joined hands and kicked up little cloud puffs on the sandy road. She looked back at their house then down at me. "Do you know what Sylvia did in the kitchen?" she whispered. "She lifted her skirt and showed me that she had lost all her hair down there." We both scrunched our noses and giggled at the odd behavior, she adding "What a strange visit!" For some reason I didn't add Romeo's ugliness but felt a gap between Mother and me. I tightened my grip around her fingers.

PEARL

Sylvia's sister was our elementary school bus driver. She and her husband would visit after church on Sunday and we'd be invited up to sit on the porch and have cookies and iced tea. Bob was getting ever so skilled at dodging stuff like this so as the only kid I was not required to participate in conversation and therefore could let my mind roam freely.

Pearl was the biggest woman I had ever seen. Her body hung over the wide driver's seat on both sides and she rose up over six feet. Her husband happened to be a small man of about 5'6' and skinny. The joke by the older kids was that he had to tether himself or he'd fall in. I didn't know what that meant for the longest time.

At work her hair was kept bobby pinned tight to her head and she barked readily at anyone who gave her a smidgeon of trouble. A bra strap was often hanging down over an enormous bicep and a variety of flower print cotton dresses strained to cover her up. But on these visits, her dark hair hung in long silky curls. She often wore a rich cobalt blue suit dress with black trim and a gold cross beamed against her olive neck. She was as pleasant as could be, laughing, joking and openly showing the love between her and her husband. I finally noticed she had the face of a classic Italian beauty. And when I met their sweet handsome son Johnny, I saw the perfect combination of them both.

Sylvia would buzz around nervously, incessantly tending to each of our needs while Romeo slumped in his chair, that awful brown juice in the corner of his frown. Mother, Pearl and her husband would gab away while I rolled around in the grass watching some imaginary scene play out up above, a favorite pastime. After these visits became a regular thing, Pearl would wink and flash a little smile at me as I got on or off the bus. All I ever saw from then on was the Sunday Pearl and I relished our special closeness.

WASTED ENERGY

Sylvia wasn't the only woman in the neighborhood with enormous energy. Mary Atkinson was another. Her husband Hank was a retired train engineer and he spent every day in his lounge chair in the front yard soaking up the sun. Mary spent most of her days sitting at the kitchen table nervously playing game after game of Solitaire. Their house was also spotless, but bright and sunny. A favorite story was that she had only spent $7.00 on doctor's fees in her entire life and that was from stitches for a finger cut.

I loved them both, but adored Mr. Atkinson and he always seemed genuinely glad to see me. I'd get all gussied up in my red ballerina suit and dance around him in the yard while we talked about happy things. Sometimes he'd nod off for a quick nap and I'd pass the time rolling around doing somersaults, cartwheels and failing at handstands until he woke back up. After an operation, he came home with a faucet sticking out of his side. He Groucho'd his eyebrows and told me it was so he didn't have to get up if he was thirsty.

His life was all about relaxation but Mary and Sylvia… they always seemed like race cars up on blocks, their engines revving. Adding to Mary's frustration, Hank died in her 73rd year and 72 was the cut off age to apply for a driver's license in Florida. She told Mother that her husband had never allowed her to drive and now she was too old, even though she was fit as a fiddle. That hit me wrong. How could he not 'allow' her to drive? And what did her being 73 have to do with her ability to drive? I learned when I was eight. I saw

Mary and Sylvia as caged birds but was confused about how they got in there and why they stayed since the door seemed to be wide open. I have since learned a thing or two about such situations...

D...EVILS

The neighbor kids I mentioned earlier about being problematic were the Johnson boys. The family consisted of Ray and his three teen-aged boys, Eddie, Andy, Chuckie and the younger daughter Sandy. Sandy was alright, but the rest of them were Satan's spawn. I don't know what happened to the Mother. Maybe she went out for the infamous pack of cigarettes or they had her stuffed in a trunk somewhere. Andy had potential but being the middle one he was always caught up in whatever evil lunacy was being pulled and all three ended up doing some serious jail time. Sandy probably married the first boy to wink at her just to escape. Whatever her method, I hope she made it out.

The first in a long list of nightmarish acts was heard when Ray came over to 'borrow' an entire loaf of bread for their dinner sandwiches. He couldn't stop laughing as he told us that Eddie and Chuckie had just burned a nest of live baby birds. The image still haunts me when it shows up in my memory flip book. They also used to sic their Pit-bull on our cat. He once dove right through the porch door screen, barely saving himself. Somehow, our tough little guy was never caught and lived a long and cared for life.

We all happened to be at Lake Jovita (or Clear Lake) one afternoon and Eddie noticed a rogue cement block in the weeds. Rogue cement blocks were everywhere in Florida then. He decided Bob needed a swimming lesson so he and his brothers tied it to his ankle and pushed him off the deep end of the dock. Fortunately, Bob had already learned to swim so he made it to the surface with only minor struggles. Racing home to the Flintstones one afternoon, I noticed a bunch of clothes and things in my 'field' home. The boys had thrown all of their sisters' belongings outside, including her bed. I hated to imagine what else was happening to her, especially after she showed up at the bus stop one morning with a broken arm.

Displaying their horns wasn't immediate though, so when Ray popped over within the first few weeks of their arrival to invite us to a fundraiser at his workplace, we had no reason to think it would be nothing but a good time. It turned out to be just that and Ray got to show off his (fake) charm and sense of humor that went along with his rugged good looks. The entertainment included a chorus line of men dressed as women doing a kick line in a comically failed attempt at unison. We contributed to Ray's costume by volunteering one of our rubber balls, cutting it in half to fill out his bra. We got a real kick and even felt a little bond when one of them fell out on stage and he winked at us.

Shortly after that, he and my Mother went out to dinner. This would be the first time she accepted a date since Dad died and she got all dolled up in her fancy blue and white dress, form fitting with a stylish neckline. I zipped her up and fastened her necklace. She put on a little make up and sprayed 'Ambush' on both of us. There were decades between us but right then, we were both young women feeling that electric charge of life.

Chuckie was maybe 14 and volunteered to babysit, for me mainly as Bob was already 10. I still slept in my crib as I had a habit of falling out from thrashing around. Not quite asleep, I heard my door open and Chuckie came in. He stood over my crib and stared at me for what seemed like forever, then unzipped his pants and pulled out his hairy pee part which was pointing right at me. He started to move his hand back and forth when Bob walked by. Fortunately, stupid Chuckie had left the door open. Bob was four years younger and half his size, but the hall light spotlighted how commanding he became as he ordered Chuckie out of my room and out of the house.

He left without incident and Bob (my Hero once again) let me stay up with him for some TV, both of us snuggled under a blanket on the divan. When the car pulled up we went to the back door to greet Mother as usual. Through the jalousie panes we saw Ray laughing his head off and Mother crying. He barely let her get out of the car before driving off. No question about me being up, she went straight to her room and closed the door. We could hear her sobbing as Bob got me down for the night. She never told us what happened, but from then on we stayed away from them and soon after they began to reveal their true ugliness. It was pure relief for the whole neighborhood when they finally moved away. I've never had one kind thought about Ray Johnson since that night and am confident that I would have smiled to learn of his passing.

SEX and HORSES (NO...)

Julie Anderson was the only other permanent kid in the neighborhood but since she was a few years older than Bob I didn't play or see that much of her. Her parents, Patty and Tex, were Mother's friends. Patty got her good looks from her half Native American Mother and had a personality of quiet acceptance. That's what was needed as Tex was just a big block of meat. Buzz cut hair, no neck, his rough voice rarely said anything bright. They vacationed in Mexico once and were over at Frank and Dolores' house telling us all about it. I had a hard time holding my then adult tongue when I heard him complain that "They don't even speak English down there!" Patty just smiled and looked out the window.

Julie took after her Mother in the looks department, but fortunately had a spirit and backbone. She was a true beauty with dark hair and eyes, little curls at each corner of her mouth and a nose that crinkled in that adorable way when she laughed. She had a gorgeous black horse which they kept on their two and half acres and they would race through the orange groves and everywhere else looking like the cover of a romance novel.

I'm a fool around horses. Scared of their size and have never been fully convinced that they want our fat butts sitting on them, even though I can see the perfect pairing. Julie's horse stepped on my foot once which didn't help my fears. My first ride was from Dade City to San Antonio (Florida that is, about seven miles) and I had no idea about guidance signals so my horse walked the whole way. No one showed me how to tighten the saddle either so I kept sliding sideways, falling completely off once. My second and last ride was similar. My friend Mark put me on one he said was so calm ten kids at a time could ride smooth on him. Having ten kids on his back tells you how big this guy was. My head was practically in the clouds and there was no saddle, tight or loose, to sit on. I hung on to his mane, all the while fearing I was angering him by doing so. My foot would accidentally tell him to gallop and for short distances terror ripped through my body until Mark stopped him. Mark, a cowboy by trade, was unimpressed.

It was a sad day despite my fears when Julie's horse died from eating Deadly Nightshade, the wild plant with purple berries somehow related to tomatoes.

One evening we were at the Anderson's for supper. The three of us kids were out back, her horse still alive and watching the games from behind the clothesline he was tied to. I was rolling around on the ground as usual and Julie had some sort of agenda with Bob. She kept knocking him down and sitting on him, poking him and pulling his hair, all the while her hips were moving all over his. He seemed to be enjoying it and didn't put up much of a fight. They probably played that game a lot more than I ever knew.

Inside, the grown-ups had a plan to dupe me. I didn't like meatloaf and Mother wanted to change that. I'm not sure why the bother as I ate everything else she put in front of me and then some, but the wheels were in motion. Patty had read that if you disguise the food the fooled child might discover a taste for it. Deciding the best costume for this meatloaf was as a Popsicle (???), they were all smiles as I downed my 'dessert'. What a wide eye…

Julie experimented with her roiling hormones on me once during a rare babysitting. We were in Mother's room with the full length mirror. I was in my coloring book on the bed while Julie was girating, watching the new rounding shapes of her body. She told me to close my eyes for a surprise which turned out to be placing my hand on her mound, now sprouting hair. My eyes popped open at the sensation and I jerked my hand away. She just laughed and continued her naked dance in front of the mirror, unconcerned with me to my relief.

They moved over the hill to a place with a lot more land so two more horses could move in. Tex acquired a group of hunting dogs which he kept in a small pen with a cement floor that he hosed out not often enough. I hated seeing those poor dogs pace back and forth in their cell when we went over for dinner.

Patty's Mother always joined us and she was a fine one. Her eyes still had life's passion in them and her laugh was genuine and hearty. She was a beauty but she had the most wrinkles I had ever seen on anyone so far and much deeper than Edna Hoster's. It was more fascinating than anything else at those dinners and I put effort into making her laugh.

SEX and a DOG (YES...)

And now introducing Judy, our Springer Spaniel mix. Sandy and Judy were the extremely tall, beautiful, genius daughters of Alex and Elizabeth, Mother's close friends over the hill, hence the pet naming honor. I was out in the back yard hanging up clothes and something caught my eye in the grove over by Baily Hill. A black and white blur was racing directly toward me. I've been injured twice by dogs, but both were still in the future so I wasn't looking at this with fear, especially since she looked more like Snoopy than a threat. Anyway, here she comes bounding straight for me through the back fields like the teenager that she was, latches on to my leg and starts furiously humping away. She knocked me down and I got those unstoppable giggles that end up hurting your stomach. Mother and Bob came running out to see what the ruckus was, watched as she humped her way up and off my body and they caught the giggles too. After that, she wanted to play and nuzzle. She became one of the family right then and along with the normal miracles dogs bring into one's life, she continued to provide the 'x' rated entertainment for years to come. She had already been spayed and the vet explained to us that since this happened before she had her first litter, she still had those urges. Most of the animals I've had since have also been spayed before their first litter and none of them were as hump happy as Judy, but we bought the explanation at the time so her behavior was accepted as is.

A particularly special moment had Bob on the living room floor watching a football game. I had just let Judy in and she immediately jumped on his feet and started humping her way up, bringing on those giggles, paralyzing both of us. She kept going right up over his Face and rolled off him right on to the floor. I think we laughed right through halftime…heck, I'm laughing right now just thinking about it.

Judy was a great dog. A big personality as you would expect, but gentle with other animals and people and she'd let us use her as a pillow when we'd watch TV at night. Bob kept her after Mother was taken and I got sent away and I got to live with her again up until she died. My dog Lenny would have been her perfect mate. Maybe they're together today, Lenny stopping people with that 'look' and Judy jumping them for a quick one. Just a fun thought.

MMMmmm…FAST FUD

The schooling part of my elementary years wasn't nearly as important to me as the people and adventures that I encountered. Lots of high IQ's in my family and friends so I was quick to catch on and therefore got bored fast. Not that I caused any real trouble in class but my constant talking proved to be problematic. (Still does.) I also had a weird behavioral issue outside of class that was never diagnosed. I probably would have been heavily medicated, dulling or altering various brain activities, as in today's world. This 'quirk' lasted until about third grade, hence the crib. Every night I would either pound my head into the pillow or roll back and forth while loudly humming. One night I woke up and found Mother, Elizabeth and Alex watching me. There was some concern on their part for a while but the problem eventually subsided on its own.

That behavior may have been attributed to the endless energy I seemed to have, perhaps powered by the massive amount of food I inhaled. It may not have happened at all if my bedtime was an hour later. I still have to stay up until my eyes are closing or I end up tossing and turning. Both Bob and I were blessed with long lasting energy as kids, perhaps because we weren't sugar kids. We had our share of desserts but we loved our spaghetti and sandwiches, stuff like that. Keeps you going much longer and without that crazy sugar rush/wipe out. Oh, jeez, do you remember those canned Hormel tamales? We had a phase with those horrible things. I tasted them once as an adult. I truly believe they're filled with dog food.

That reminds me…. a famous fast food restaurant named for its taco-like offerings over by Busch Gardens in Tampa got shut down once for having an 'inordinate amount' of dog food cans in its dumpster. And dinner is served.

MY BEST FRIEND

Bob and I played together all the time and occasionally scared Mother half to death. Bob had a big closet along the back wall of his bedroom that had a bamboo curtain instead of a door. Mother came into the room to put some clothes away and saw a flame through that curtain. She found us sitting on the shoe shelf lighting matches just inches away from the bottom of his hanging clothes. "Hi Mommy!"

Bob had a fun little game of his own. Every so often as he faced Mother, he would look just past her and say "It's the Big-Big!" She finally figured out that it was her shadow and it became cute, but those first few heart stopping times…?

One of my own indoor games was playing secretary at Mother's desk. I have a beautiful old oak desk now and every now and then that same child/adult (adult/child now) feeling comes on when I'm organizing my files or whatever. Anyway, one day Bob and I were drawing a bird together and something just wasn't right. Finally it hit us that we had drawn the legs backwards, knees bending forward like a human. That took us down, we were laughing so hard. In my thirties, I had a cat named Moto, for her mo' toes on each foot. We were in the house that my soon to be boyfriend would burn down and Moto was walking toward Bob across the table. I said, "Moto, kiss Bob's elbow" and she did! That had us going for a while, too. Sharing the same sense of humor with someone is such a treat. The littlest thing can bring howls of laughter and the mental connection of seeing something the exact same way is beyond close. These times were few and far between later on, but we stacked up a million of them in early years and I treasure each one.

Bob decided I should know how to put out fire with sand. He was always teaching me handy stuff like that. Mr. Thorpe, a retired builder from the next road over, had given him an official carpenter's apron which he adored and wore constantly. He told me to get a handful of sand and throw it when he lit the bottom of the apron. "Okay, the apron's on fire, now throw the sand!" Obediently I threw it, not on the fire but over to the left. Being the knowledgeable Boy Scout, he dropped and rolled extinguishing the flames immediately. It took a minute for us both to appreciate what had happened but once we did...

Bob was an excellent big brother in those years. I can't remember ever fighting and he never excluded me as some older siblings do. We always picked each other for teams and still had a blast when it was just the two of us. Along with the driving lessons, he taught me croquet, how to shoot pool, play baseball and scores of other things. He defended me on the bus and where ever else was needed. I knew he always had my back. Maybe that's why I didn't feel the lack of a dad back then as much as I could have.

One day during a round of croquet in our front yard, our friend Nina Sue hit him square in the forehead with a mallet during her back swing. She was a big girl with a big swing and it knocked him flat on his back. I raced over and watched as a red crescent moon formed, the inside dented in. I actually felt some of his pain.

He seemed to be the one to take on most of the physical hurting between the two of us. I did give myself a black eye once when still in head banging mode, smashing my face right into the handle of a roll away I was sleeping on. And a neighbor kid threw a croquet ball from close range directly into my face. The absolute blankness in her eyes as she threw it was the scarier part of that deal. As our lives progressed, Bob would feel more physical pain, I would feel more fear.

SCHOOL?

Hhhhmmmm, didn't I mention school? Never went to kindergarten as I already knew how to read, write and 'rithmatic and my birthday fell in December so I entered first grade at five years old. My poor Mother endured my howling sobs every day for weeks on end during the drive there. As soon as I got out of the car, I would dry up and skip merrily down the corridor to my class.

Mother and I were talking with two of the first grade teachers, Mrs. Ward and Mrs. Reedy, on the outside corridor one morning. Mrs. Reedy was with a little boy, his back hugged up to her. One of her giant boobs was resting on his head like half risen bread dough. It was all I could do to keep from laughing but neither adult seemed to notice. I imagine that little boy turned out to be a real boob man and/or possibly a highly contented baker. Anyway, the rest of the year was a bore, taking unnecessary naps after lunch and smelling rotting sandwiches from Mary Don's desk.

Second grade was Mrs. McNeil's class. Her husband worked at the Coca-Cola factory in town and every one of her students got a tiny case of coke at the end of the year. Bob got a wooden case with real coke in capped bottles, probably worth a small fortune now. My case was plastic and the bottles were colored glass but I still loved it and it was a perfect size for my Barbie (not at all).

Mrs. McNeil had a little general store set up in the corner of her classroom. We were asked to bring in empty food containers to fill the shelves. We'd all take turns working the cash register and making change, reading labels and restocking, dealing with and being customers and a host of other academic and social skills. Pure genius on her part.

My tomboy came out big and strong in the third grade. Paul, Carlton and I were the biggest kids in class, outweighing everyone else by a good 10-30 pounds. The class picture shows me daintily hunched over my desk with a snarl on my face.

Mother was forced to cut my hair that year adding to my new gender appearance. She discovered I was only brushing the top layer when a huge knot poked through at the nape of my neck. Deciding to comb it out for me, she found my neck to be a dingy gray from lack of washing. Chop, chop, my hair was as short as any boys' and my baths were annoyingly monitored.

My job on the playground was to chase down the boys and sit on them while the other girls kissed them, a role which suited me just fine. Those poor frail boys gasping for air while being mauled. It's a wonder any of us reach a sane adulthood.

My monkey chatter came out big and strong this year as well. Our report card was divided into six grading sections. The first one says, "Anne is a very good student, but she has a tendency to talk too much." Second section "Anne catches on quickly but her talking is somewhat disruptive at times" and so on until the last section simply reads "She talks too much!"

Our teacher had us go outside on a chilly afternoon to brush our teeth and then chew a red pill which would show us the food still left behind. Of course there was red everywhere and we were happily stretching our faces like chimps showing our disgusting mouths to each other when it started snowing! It only lasted a short while, but it was wild for us cracker kids.

President Kennedy was killed during this year. I was sitting on one of the benches built around the trees near the basketball court. A teacher ran out on to the playground openly crying and shrieked, "The President's been shot! The President's been shot!" The entire playground went into stop action then burst into tears and screams. Kids of all ages were falling down, hugging or running in circles unaware of what to do with the emotions that had just taken over their little bodies. Whether or not they knew exactly what, everyone sensed something truly terrible had happened. Libby, the older volunteer who was sitting next to me, convulsively sobbed until she had to be led back to the nurse. It was pure madness as I'm sure anyone will tell you who lived through it.

SOME GOOD-LOOKIN' HILLBILLIES

The Blackburn family came down from the hills of North Carolina this year and moved into a house way out in the country but on my bus route. Mary, the youngest, was in my class. I was seven, she was twelve, but we were of similar size and acted more like the boys so we quickly became pals. All the kids looked alike having smooth tan skin and blonde hair with a kind smile. I was 'in love' with her older brother Joe for a while. Academic brains were not a large part of their makeup but there is much a brain has to offer. Generous and friendly with loads of common sense, any of them could have fixed whatever came their way and could tell you how to prevent the problem in the future. They attracted like friends and Freddie Shepard was Joe's best pal. Freddie was a tall, handsome senior, caring and gentle. He taught me how to slow dance while I stood on his feet. I DID love him.

Mary's older sister Ruby was 17, married and lived across the dirt road from the main house with her husband who was twice her age. She looked exactly like Daisy Mae in the L'il Abner cartoons, just a bustin' out all over and long blonde curls falling over some of it.

The boys all talked very slowly. David would say "Aah dawn't knaww" like dripping molasses and that pearl was immediately filed under 'must readily use' in our comedy drawer. Bob and I said it that way for decades for grins and later as a mood lightener during our argumentative phone calls. I always liked visiting the Blackburns. They offered so many differences.

Well, to be honest, I could have done without seeing one little habit. We were up in the hayloft and Mary was hanging over the edge making some weird noise. I went over to see what was what and found her cleaning out her nose by closing off one side and blowing through it. I started gagging uncontrollably, nearly throwing up and reeling around the floor. To this day, I have a similar reaction when I see someone blowing or hacking something up and as is the humor of the universe, I tend to see it a lot. I've even had to pull off the road from a particularly violent gag reaction.

One day Mary and I were talking about sex, what little I could contribute, and with complete innocence she said that her brother had "broke her in". I wasn't quite sure what that meant so she explained in a factual tone that one of her brothers was chosen to make sure that her first time with a man would go well so that it wouldn't hurt and she shouldn't expect any less from future boyfriends. My eight years took this in as best as I could. The well-meaning side of it did come through to me, but Yikes! Double Yikes!

The bus ride livened considerably when the Blackburns joined the group. The Redmonds were renting the house across the street adding another five kids and we all got along really well. Frank, small in build but already a man, made up the third of the kindly trio with Joe and Freddie. Debbie, Mary and I were pals and her older sister Donna provided a different kind of entertainment. She was 'man hungry' and she filled her plate every time and place she could. I caught her on the bus with her boyfriend Denny's hand up her skirt and her reaction was a wink and a smile. When the Beatles made their debut on the Ed Sullivan show, we invited the Redmonds over to watch and Donna practically lost her mind. She was just like those girls in the audience, screaming, crying and bouncing off the wall making it seem like we were right there in the front row!

There were a few bullies on the bus but too young to be really harmful. Tommy, the boy genius from over the hill, took care of one kid by calling him 'Amoeba Brain'. His confusion at the unknown word left him powerless.

ADVENTURES IN BABYSITTING

I baby sat for a spoiled brat on our side of the hill only once. The parents already had two boys well into their twenties. Jack, a real life Ben Cartwright, gave his wife the present of a new baby as she neared her 50th birthday which turned her into a nervous bird like creature, eyes bulging and wings flapping. She answered any problem the kid threw at her with either a toy or sugar. They had cattle and grove money and the kid's room looked like a department store. He was maybe six and had his own TV, phone, record player and whatever that day's toy commercial was hocking.

We went outside to look at a cow penned in a trailer and Brat-o decided to poke at her with a stick. She was getting irritated and I opened my mouth to tell him to stop. Splat! The cow kicked part of a pie right in my face. The kid had to pay. After a quick chase, I caught him and locked him in the basement until his crying turned into an apology, which took over an hour. I was talking to him from the other side of the door the whole time and the basement was finished complete with pool table, but I did turn out the light so I may have added an emotional scar to his life.

No more babysitting for me, good for all concerned as my maternal instinct never really reached its full bloom. Running into the kid later in life, he was the snobby, shallow guy I expected. I do feel sorry for people raised like that, but it's not easy. Not a lot of good comes from having too much.

I may not have the full maternal instinct but I do tend to stick up for the weak, picked on, or the underdog and David B. was the poster boy for all three. He and his younger brother obviously shared their parents' DNA, but David was more like a caricature of Larry. He was a human rabbit. Giant ears stuck straight out from his head, huge round darting eyes set in a long thin face and the unfortunate icing, his two large front teeth actually extended a bit over his bottom lip. I hovered around his skinny little self whenever possible but there was no stopping the endless taunting. A cold morning brought on a barrage of painful ear flicks. Mr. Reffuse, (actual name!) our sadistic 7th grade algebra teacher, made fun of him right in class. Once while sitting behind David, I felt a warm wetness on one of my Keds and realized he had just pee'd his pants. Knowing the beast teacher would embarrass him for the normal bodily function we all have, he tried to hold it til class ended. I followed right behind him out the door. Evil

Reffuse thankfully missed his chance but I can't say what other kids in the bathroom may have done. David never really spoke much, his speech impediment bringing on further belittling, but I did make him laugh occasionally which brought some joy to both of us.

THE SILENT SNAKE EATS THE FLOWER POT LADIES

Mother was becoming disillusioned with the Methodist church we were going to. It became clear to her that it was more of a social center than a place to discuss what a real Christian should be. She had always described herself as Agnostic... on the fence, but wanting to hop off and she wasn't getting what she needed at this church to jump into the greener pasture. The minister was a good man but weary of spouting the same sermons and too tired to jazz up his delivery. Snoring was often heard in the congregation. It was the coffee/cookie gathering afterward that brought people in, mainly the rich ladies. Mother and I used to call them Flower Pot Ladies because of their attire. Every Sunday was an unofficial contest between who could balance the largest floral arrangement on their heads or show off the most petals in the print of their dresses.

Mother and I continued to go for a few more years, trying to ignore the contests; who traveled more or farther, promotions at work (their husbands, not their own), whose children were besting whose... and those flowers. They all looked so silly to me. We would sing along with the hymns and listen to the minister as best we could, but more interesting things like the laundry kept popping up right at church time to redirect our attention.

We were coming up to the tracks on Church Str. after a notably wasted Sunday morning, both of us quiet in our boredom. Suddenly the train was right in front of us. Mother slammed on the brakes just feet from the giant metal snake as it silently slithered through town, never once announcing itself. So close we could see only the bottom half, the cars inched by. I doubt I had a thought in my head but fear and awe, but later that afternoon Mother made the final decision that listening to a group of petty snobs was not needed to become a more caring and considerate person, so No More Church.

EUPHEMIA, EZEKIEL and ENORMOUS EDIFICATION

Mrs. Euphemia Rowland was my fourth grade teacher. She was a few decades older than my Mother but they became friends outside of school. Kind people tend to recognize each other and the outer shell becomes transparent. She always had a sweet smile on her sweet wrinkled face and a thin sweater over her shoulders held together in front with a variety of fancy butterfly clips. The small gold cross around her neck occasionally rode outside the buttoned up white blouse with the Peter Pan collar. A dark skirt, not too tight or too full went below the knee and flat comfortable shoes completed her outfit. Her hair was from the same era as her name having a fat roll across the shoulders and a smaller one across her forehead. A hairnet held everything in place. This was the way she looked every single day that I knew her, with the uncharacteristic change of hair color, from dark brown to a lighter shade and even red a few times. Everyone has a little sumpin'-sumpin' going on.

Can't say I remember the entire years' worth of her teachings, but there are a few particulars that remain with me today. She and I were talking on the playground one day and while looking at my fingernails she stated "You have lovely moons" informing me that they are a good way to keep a check on your health. If they stay clear and well-shaped, odds are not much is wrong. If one becomes deformed or lines or colors appear in the nail, you might want to get a check-up. I believe that 'old wives tale' has been medically proven now and I do keep an eye on them. A friend noticed a black line in one of hers and soon after was diagnosed with breast cancer. (She's fine now).

We learned our times tables in her class. Up to twelve times twelve, that is. Anything after that requires thought. Had we spent the year doing nothing but times tables, I could tell you what $6970324581 \times 9386541072$ was in one blink. But since we stopped where we did, we had time to diagram sentences, do long division, discover the aerial viewpoint (handy and entertaining) and some other random things. Did you know there is 'a rat' in separate, but not in desperate? The word 'unquestionably' holds all the vowels. I impressed my

Uncle Frank with that knowledge on his birthday that same year. Why on Earth did we have to read the hideous story of Ezekiel the Raccoon that when caught in a farmer's trap had to chew off his own foot to escape?

This was also the year those dreadfully inaccurate American history books came into play with Pocahontas, Captain John, and the rest of the original Brady Bunch all getting along so splendidly. We put on an equally truth hiding play about Columbus, Magellan and a few other hijackers, rapists and murderers. Oh sorry, I meant explorers. The simple plot was that 'the Queen' (me again?) sat in the middle of the stage while the other 'explorers' asked permission for their cultural genocide plans. Oh sorry, I meant cultural genocide plans.

A week or so before show time we were in the classroom discussing the play while decorating for the Holidays. I was standing on the book shelves that ran along the wall under the bank of windows that together formed the entire back wall. (Our school was of very good design.) As I taped construction paper leaves to the panes of glass, Mrs. Euphemia Rowland offhandedly mentioned that she had a friend whose daughter was "CHUBBY LIKE YOU" and had the perfect dress for my role. The entire class looked up at my pudgy frame silhouetted by the light and burst into laughter. I'm sure she felt terrible about it, but my hot face was not concerned with HER feelings just yet. Not in the standard curriculum, but I did gain a richer awareness of how a crushing humiliation can feel.

The wall of windows allowed the three remaining solid walls to carry lots of maps, cork boarding for announcements, drawings, etc. with one entire wall covered in chalk boards. Above these were big green cards printed with the Alphabet. They were in most classrooms, as knowing how to read, write and spell had more importance then it sometimes seems to have today. I mention these letters because in a current friend's elementary class one of the letters was upside down and that's the way he learned it to be. I noticed it in a recent writing and pointing it out, it not only annoyed him, but he didn't believe me. I saw it as being helpful, not as insult or criticism. Yes, I'm one of those people who will tell you when you have a booger showing or you mispronounce a word and I would certainly hope that a friend would tell me if my skirt was tucked into my drawers before a stranger does. Once a friend let me go through our day together with the infamous spinach in my teeth because she "Didn't want to embarrass me (by telling me!)." That logic I don't understand.

Considering that I'm a know-it-all, smarty pants comedian type, I have found that laughing at myself before the public onset helps to ease that crushing humiliation and any other emotional stabbings one might encounter. I'm fully aware that I make an ass of myself on a regular basis. Depending on the situation or mood, I can be socially awkward and feel/act as though caged when put on the spot. I can also feel incredibly close to someone within a short time and blurt out some deep truth, shocking my new friend into throwing some bricks up on their inner wall. I have lost focus more times than I care to remember and shoved my overly heightened priorities into bewildered faces. We all do things we wish we could take back, but we must not let these incidences rule our lives. My Mother's way... deal with it and move on.

Uh oh, the thread slipped from my needle again, sorry.

One day a new kid appeared in class named Jerry Brooks. Quiet kid with dark hair and eyes is what I noticed. Euphemia Rowland noticed his shabby clothes and bare feet. A few days later after school, Euphemia Rowland, my Mother, Jerry and I went to Otto's Dept. store and fit him with a pair of shoes, cost split three ways. Otto was a good man. That same week in the grocery store, Mother added huge bags of rice and flour, monster amounts of hamburger and giant cans of this and that into our cart. She brushed away any real explanation when I asked and went about emptying the store of 'FAMILY' sized items.

Back seat filled, we started driving the wrong way home. Why we weren't speaking about this was puzzling as the two of us talked about everything. Looking out the passenger window, asphalt became dirt, houses became cattle and then everything became orange grove. We parked near one of a dozen small wooden shacks and soon a young woman came out. Long dark blond waves of hair surrounded her lovely face, but her eyes showed...no hope?

My Mother seemed embarrassed and tripping over her words of "I thought you might like some food" began handing the bags over to the woman. I noticed the small windows in their 'home' were filled with young faces when two of them slipped away and came out to help, both looking a lot like Jerry Brooks. When the last bag was handed over, the woman and my Mother spoke with their eyes, smiled quietly and turned back to their own lives.

On the way home Mother explained that the young woman lived there with her husband and eight children. Her husband picked produce for a living and they traveled from grove to farm, living in whatever was provided for the workers. The oldest child was already a picker, having dropped out of school, and the rest would follow suit as soon as they were able, eventually including the Mother. The money would improve with each added pair of hands but right now they needed help. And that was that. The facts were laid bare for me to think about the way things were always told to me. The whole thing was massively influential.

Another example of my Mother's to the bone impacts happened during an Easter egg hunt. She was good at hiding and there were always a few we would never find. This Easter I had decided to 'fix' that and in the night hunted them down. Morning came and Bob bubbled joyously, mentally honing his detective skills. I was excited because I knew where the eggs were and would 'win'.

After a quick breakfast it was game time. I lifted the record player top to retrieve the first egg and zoomed over to the divider for the beer stein. Across the room, the porcelain skunk family gave up their quarry, then I snatched the one resting atop the Bennett Cerf joke book in the bookcase.

Within minutes, my basket was full. "Well, that's over", Mother said flatly and walked out of the room. Bob stood crumbling, his fun stolen. Her three words highlighted Bob's deflating stance and the devilish fingers of my actions gripped my brain. She was good, my Mother.

THE 'SITUATION'

We weren't Jerry Brooks poor, but we were still considered poor. I wouldn't have known had my 'Problems of American Democracy' teacher not laid out a graph saying that a family of four living on $4000.00 a year was considered poverty level. This was 1972. I immediately rebuked him by stating strong and loud that my Mother, brother and I had lived on my father's $3000.00 social security for as long as I could remember and we were never in poverty. The whole class went silent and my teacher (who I loved dearly) was at a loss for words and changed the subject. Being poor is not a crime or a disease. It's a situation.

During our 'situation', Mother volunteered as a Gray Lady in the hospital. I suppose her Parkinson's prevented her from getting hired in a paying job, but she still wanted to be useful. And as I said, she managed well what money she did have. We had a brown and white '59 Ford Fairlaine until we moved to town, then upgraded to an aqua '63 Ford Galaxie. Both cars were very snazzy I thought, but the aqua one...Wow! It was just like that model of the Thunderbird convertible I put together (not at all). We even got the living room furniture reupholstered once. Poor people don't get to do that. I know that as I am now an upholsterer.

We got new school clothes at the beginning of each year and plenty of food if I had anything to do with it. I had no pride whatsoever in that department. The school lunch served an out of this world peanut butter brownie not nearly often enough. I would go from kid to kid asking "You gonna eat that?" "You gonna eat that?" "You gonna eat that?" and did not stop until I got at least ten. Still showing signs of that trait in my early twenties, I attended a Thank You party with my boyfriend who had led the crew that built the host's new house. A lavishly laden table held a bowl of marinated Brussels sprouts, a new dish and a new concept for me. Thinking this a rare opportunity, I managed to slyly consume the entire bowl. I later found out that the recipe was simply a box of frozen sprouts and some bottled Italian dressing, but this was before I learned about real food and was not about to let this exotic dish get away. I still get big joy from coming across new foods but have managed to get my 'Miss Piggy' under control.

I was maybe eight or nine when a special Christmas gave me a Cathy doll. She was three feet tall and if I held her hand she could walk with me. Needless to say, we spent a lot of time together. Bob had gotten an old faded red VW bug somehow and was fixing it up for when he could legally drive. Cathy and I would sit in it and have long conversations or thumb through Playboys for jokes while smoking Bob's cherry flavored Cigarillos he had stashed in the glove box. He never got mad at me for that or for anything else for that matter. After his hormones kicked in, he did go through a phase of beating the Holy Hell out of me but that ended as soon as I found out what hurts a boy the most. It only took one major twist and that nonsense stopped.

CHANGES

Mother had the first of her two operations for Parkinsons' Disease during the summer of my fourth and fifth grade. The night before the surgery all the patients in the ward had their heads shaved and painted with that orange mercurochrome. Mother joked that they looked like a basket of Easter eggs. She was like the father in the movie "Life is Beautiful" that way, taking the fear out of things.

Bob and I stayed with Dolores and Frank. They were still living in the same ranch house having converted the carport into their master bedroom, the three boys now in the two original bedrooms. They were our closest relatives, we loved each other and had tons of fun, but living there brought about some new and unnerving conditions for me.

First, it was a man who doled out the punishment instead of a woman. I loved my uncle dearly, he was the King of Cornball, was openly and madly in love with Dolores (seeing none of that at home I drank this in), adored his children and was a fine man over all, but in those days he had a ferocious temper fueled by a bottomless thermos of coffee and his boys tested it on a regular basis. Back then, it was considered appropriate to whip the tar out of your kid when they acted up and having been an occasional witness, I had a healthy fear when I saw that particular shadow darken his face.

One day I caused an accidental 'No-No' and terror swept over me. I ran into the bedroom I was sharing with the two youngest boys and slid under the bottom bunk bed. The crime discovered, tears welled up as I heard my name being called out. I was far too scared to answer, so I scrunched as flat into the wall as I could possibly get. Neighbors soon got involved and my frazzled family members were running all over calling out my name. Once, Frank even looked under the bed, but fear had made me invisible.

It seemed like hours later when an arm reached under and pulled me out, a spring end ripping across my arm. I was sobbing and shaking like a leaf, my eyes as wide as dinner plate Dahlias. Frank was more relieved than angry at this point so the whipping never came, just a bunch of hugs from everyone and a lecture about owning up to your actions, but I became acutely aware that summer as to what might tic him off.

Sharing a room and with stinky boys (still loved them both) was also a big difference. My cousin Alan was born with some kind of leg problem, so at night he had to wear braces that had a connecting bar at the ankle about two feet long, keeping his legs straight and apart. The poor kid slept on his side, so one leg was always sticking up in the air. Whatever that contraption was, it worked. Dale had the bottom bunk and maybe I slept in the toy box. I don't remember but toys were all over the floor along with dirty dishes and sweaty boy clothes. My room at home was very orderly and didn't smell like anything at all. It was a long summer in this regard.

Dolores was ruler of all households needs. The cleaning, laundry, meals, shopping, doling out the money; she did everything. She even ventured into the boys rooms now and then to collect the old food dishes.

At home, we were doing our own laundry before we were ten. It was kind of fun because we had one of those hand cranked machines like a pasta machine that had rollers to feed the clothing through. We also cleaned the bathroom, vacuumed and washed the windows. All three of us did our share which seemed only right, but I hated those jalousie windows. Narrow glass panes held together by a maze of aluminum that was really hard to vacuum around. And there was always a spider family or some other giant beast hiding in there somewhere.

Dolores would make everyone their own specific breakfasts on the weekend. And she would whistle or sing while she did it. She had an operatic voice and her whistles came out in the same big vibrato, high toned and strong. It was something to be proud of.

She and I were in the kitchen making a family favorite called Tagliarini one day when she spotted one of Frank's golf clubs sticking out from behind the freezer. Alan was nearby so she asked him to "pick it up and put it back in the bag, please", her hands busy with the macaroni. Huffing and puffing as he did this terribly back breaking task, he muttered "I work like a slave around here". Dolores and I both cracked up and that phrase joined the ever growing file under 'use for comedic purposes'.

Dolores had The Absolute Best Laugh in the World. I wish I had a recording of it because there are really no words to fully get the sound across to you. Full, rich, deep from the belly and pure of the heart is as close as I can get. The joy she was feeling resonated right through to your core through that laugh. I could have heard it every day, but life did not keep us in the same place for too long.

The family on their kitty-corner was the Barths, Norma and Roy with their kids Kenny and Billy Bob. Norma and Dolores were big pals and Norma was a real sweetheart with a ready smile and a sweet treat to go with it. She always bought the boys shorts a few sizes too big for growth spurts so they had a Minnie Marvin look going on.

We all played together, running through the neighbors' yards and with so few cars, right into the empty streets. Ours was recently asphalted, the curbs redone and now rising above the lawn they held back. The game was chase and I was in pursuit of Billy Bob, who took off toward his yard. I tripped on the curb and slid across the rough asphalt on my bare knees. Now that was some real pain and in my usual fashion, I let the entire listening area know about it. I can still see Dolores bending over me and picking out pieces of the black goo. But hey, Bactine and bandages, a bowl of ice cream with cartoon topping and I was quiet in a matter of hours. I walked like a robot for a month and had those scars for years.

Dolores always seemed to be battling her weight so when I came under wing, she was not about to allow the same suffering for me. On a diet I went and most of the extra poundage I had so diligently packed on came off. And she was my sewing teacher. I took to it quickly and began making my own school clothes. Until then, we had shopped from the chubby section in the Sears catalogue so I had a big incentive to learn. Girls were still not allowed to wear pants to school, so it was to be dresses, but they were MY dresses. I embroidered a Porky Pig on one that I'm thinking of remaking and did all sorts of other 'out of the box' stuff. What a ball! A big ole' double door opened up in my brain.

STUFFED WITH STRAW?

My hair was growing out in fifth grade and due to the weight loss I looked more like a female. During the class picture the long side of my untrained bangs fell over one eye just as the camera snapped and it looked like I was trying to be sexy. I was mercilessly teased about it and mortified. Overt sexiness has never come comfortably to me. The few times I've set out to be sexy, it was awkward and unnatural and I felt more embarrassment than anything else.

Soon into the year, our teacher Mrs. Gates announced with an ear to ear grin that she was pregnant and leaving for good. Her husband showed up on her last day looking just like Red Robertson. I loved Mrs. Gates and feared for her future. The rest of the year was a blur.

Except that is, for the paddling I got from Coach McCullough... for talking in class naturally. He was a nice guy and he and his wife even had some barbeques for the kids once in a while at their pink house with the purple door, but manohmanohmanohmanohman, those paddling's were serious! He had a long board with holes drilled through to insure a few welts. I received ten solid thwacks, some of which caught the tops of my thighs. And we weren't supposed to cry. What were kids made of back then?

It may have been this year that my friend Ricki had a sleepover at my house and Mother let us camp out in the car. After talking our heads off and probably downing a bunch of sugar, we got the idea to do some cruisin'. Middle of the night, two ten year old girls out for a stroll by the highway....what could happen? This time we were the culprits. We were walking in the big culvert beside the highway and noticed a car coming down Greer Hill. A light bulb went on and we thought it would be hysterical to lay face down in twisted positions and 'play dead'. When the car stopped, we jumped up and took off running. I'm not sure what Ricki saw, but I did happen to catch the horrified look on the woman's face in the passenger seat. What an adorable little pair we were.

Ms. Morgan and then Ms. Bentley were our gym teachers. Ms. Bentley looked like Jane Lynch and it was rumored (by the adults) that she 'lived' with a woman. Ms. Morgan was very muscular and she had dark tan flawless skin. I suppose she did carry herself in a 'manly' fashion, but she always had great games for us to play, was a comfort to a crying kid and rolled her

Most of the pictures I had of these early years were finally thrown away after the Mother of someone I barely knew found herself with a trunkful belonging to me. She kept them for years hoping we could somehow find each other. Her superb kindness has always stayed with me.

eyes along with us girls as we watched that lame pink film about our periods. We all loved her. She was fired for no reason by the adults and replaced by Ms. Bentley who eventually shared the same fate.

The summer was a basic repeat of the last, Mother having gone away for the same operation but on the other side of her brain. She was put on L-Dopa, the drug the movie 'Awakenings' was about, starring Robert DeNiro and Robin Williams. Not being a complainer, I was unaware if she had any bad side effects the first go round. A positive one from the operations and/or the drug was that she no longer needed the walker or even the cane. She even jumped a good height once when a roach scurried toward her feet. But after the second surgery, I noticed her emotions were being toyed with. I came home one day to find her crying on the sofa. That was a rare sight and I didn't know how to help. Whatever nonsense I may have said was not what she wanted to hear and she shooed me away. God, that was a terrible feeling.

AND SO IT BEGINS

Sixth grade was only slightly less blurry. 'Villager' skirts and purses made their entrance and the clics began to form. Rich kids here, all others way over there. Maybe it was my class clown status that allowed me to remain friends with the 'popular' girls because not only could we not afford those clothes, but brown plaid was not anything I wanted to wear.

This was also the first year that those 'I Like You, Do you Like Me, Check Yes or No' notes came into play. I was 'in love' with Louie Miller since the first grade and finally decided to find out how he felt about me. Curse those notes!

This was 1966, the year that John Lennon said the Beatles were more popular than Jesus, or whatever he actually said. I was over at Melinda's house with LaDonna playing records when Melinda suggested we gather all her Beatle 45's and go scrape them up on the road out front. That seemed like a waste of good music but I scraped a few before the feelings of 'wrong' and 'stupid' became too strong to contend with and I just stopped. We shared our differences of opinion and I was asked to wait on the front steps until Mother came to get me. Da, da, da, dum, the outcasting had begun.

I have never understood what people got so upset about. John Lennon was noting their worldwide popularity, not ordering us to "Follow our beliefs and no one else's" like all the accepted organized religions do.

More outcasting came with the brave Reggie Quarterman, the first black kid we had in our sixth grade class. Makes me physically ill to think of how his last name might have come about. Mother pointed out his rickety unpainted shack of a house on our way to the Kwik Chek one afternoon. I was extra nice to him after that and one day in class he snuck up from behind and kissed me on the elbow. I just laughed, but opinions were hardening in our young minds and I sensed a silent division forming from the angry stares. This was the beginning.

SECTION THREE

TENTH STREET TOWNIES

Mother found a paying job with the Headstart program after her operations allowed more mobility. My summer was spent being her volunteer. I read to the kids, made sure they brushed their teeth, watched them on the playground and generally looked after them. Too many kids at this school had never seen a toothbrush, let alone a book and I was being exposed to a new set of kid problems. A little girl daily complained of headaches until I finally figured out that her Mother was pulling her hair back too tight in the rubber band. One kid still has a place in my heart. Cute little blond boy named Daniel. FULL of energy. He was always into something and I spent a lot of time chasing him into a sweet bear hug. One day I noticed Mother, the teacher and the nurse talking quietly in the corner. The nurse took Daniel away. On the way home, Mother told me he was being taken from his parents because as punishment for his energetic ways, they would hold him by his feet, knock his head into the cement floor and lock him in a dog cage. This class was a precursor to first grade and I prayed he was taken away soon enough.

We also moved into town that summer. Seventh grade would prove more socially active and with mother's new job, she didn't want to spend her spare time schlepping me all over the place. Of course that particular word was never used. Otto was the only Jewish man in town and he kept that under his hat, which was more fedora than yarmulke. Central Fla. wasn't exactly accepting of 'others' in those days.

It wasn't until I was living in upstate New York in my early twenties that I had any real interaction with Jewish people. On my first visit to NYC's famed Katz' Delicatessen I asked for mayonnaise and turned the place to stone. When I suggested to my Jewish boss who owned the bar I tended that he 'jue' one of his suppliers down,

I simply thought it was a word that meant 'to haggle', like at a flea market or garage sale. I'd heard the word used from time to time (outside family) but no one ever added, "I say this as a slam against Jewish people because of my bigoted beliefs". Mother would have definitely enlightened me had she ever heard me use it, as would Frank and Dolores. They were members of the N.A.A.C.P. (Don't you think that title need a change up, btw?). My boss's facial expression showed shock of course, but also confusion. He was a friend and knew my words didn't come from an evil place so after explanation, I promptly removed it from my vocabulary.

Have you ever said Jerry-rigged? The term 'Jerry' is derogatory, introduced during WW1 and refers to the Germans helmets looking like a Jeroboam, or chamber pot. What about "He jipped me?" It's spelled 'gyp' and is an insult toward Gypsys who are often stereotyped as thieves.

THE HOUSE

Our new house was on the edge of one of two rich sections in town, a tiny two bedroom/one bath. It had a decent sized eat in kitchen with a smaller room off to the side for the washer/dryer and my sewing table set up, which had by now become a part of me. The living room was the fancy part. Wide floor length drapes covering both picture windows (NO jalousies!) with matching sheers and carpeting. Everything

With Uncle Frank, Judy (in the middle with me), Jacques with Mother, Alan with either Sugar or Spice

59

Left to right in back: Dale, Gregg, Bob;
in front: Anne, Alan, Mother
We had the same TV always. 13" screen and
about 20" long!

including the paint color was in varying shades of the wildly popular Avocado green. Our furniture (NOT Avocado green) fit perfectly and it was quite a luxurious feeling to be surrounded by all that fabric and softness.

The large chain linked back yard bordered the defunct railroad tracks behind the house. A line of Crepe Myrtle grew along the back and the tracks were down an embankment making them all but disappear. These tracks would soon provide a perfect escape route for my Mother's murderer.

It also came with The Garage, which turned into a much more important place than where to park the car.

PRETEEN PRIMATES

The way I saw it, the Friday and Saturday night dances were the Big Excitement in town for many of the kids. Well, there was that rumor about the entrepreneurial young lass who charged a 'contestant' ten dollars to try and pull a coke bottle out of her hoo-hah while she stood on a table in a North End biker bar. The dances were set up in part I'm sure, to drain the energy of 'Mayberrys' sons and daughters before they got to that level of entertainment. Normal wildness was to tear around in an orange grove, plow bumpers into back road STOP signs and occasionally drive on the railroad tracks in someone's beater pick-up, but they were random acts brought on by the rare six pack or jug of Bali Hai wine. It was the anticipation of the dances that kept the school corridors buzzing with flirting and fashion all week long.

Technically, Friday was for the Junior High and Saturday was for High schoolers, but no one paid attention to that. Everyone was there and everything was happening. The dance hall was right next to the bowling alley/pool room creating a lively stream of kids going back and forth making various stops along the way.

These stops were designated areas outside the buildings as Nature once again lent itself to our entertainment agenda. I was told that some of the rich popular girls were selling $4.00 blow jobs by the back hedgerow. Not sure about the money exchange, but the act was sometimes not hidden well enough for secrecy. A small stand of trees across the street by the jailhouse was for make out sessions. Kudzu had overtaken them and an entrance had been made but kept covered with an entanglement of vines. No one could see you when inside as I tried spying from a far once but to no avail. (Haha, I can hear Mother laughing when I asked her in earnest who Noah Vale was.) Horny freshmen would stand under the street lights checking out who's older brother got which kind of lucky by noting from what section of foliage they emerged.

The poor kids hung out on the picnic tables in the grassy area nearby. Present and future criminals had their shadowy back corner by the bowling alley. The girls who weren't in any of those places were in the bathroom smoking, applying yet another coat to their sorely overdone make-up, reshaping the toilet paper in their bras or sharing kissing techniques on each other's forearms.

There were separations on the dance floor as well, but much less pronounced. You could dance right next to a football star if bold enough as the lines, couples facing one another like a Victorian social, were only loosely formed by grade or friendship. My friend Linda and I would partner up and 'Monkey' our way over to the cute older boys. Ricky M. was my brother's friend. He had dark hair, full lips, kind deep brown eyes and his body chemistry brought out the best of Brut. I was nutty over him and will admit to still liking that cologne because of him. He and his athlete pals would all do 'The Alligator' at some point in the evening. This was long before break dancing and it involved undulating on the floor on your stomach. Mighty provocative for a 12 year old.

There were two sisters who shared a special talent. The younger one was my pal and I was awestruck watching her. During the drum solo (all bands did drum solos then) they would shift their bodies into twelfth gear and do a blurring full body shimmy, making their butt length hair take on a rippling waterfall effect. They could do this for several minutes and it was quite the show stopper.

Several years ago, I saw a fantastic performance by a troupe of dancer/gymnasts in our beautifully refurbished downtown theater. One member of the group took his solo and clicked around the stage like a bendable robot, various parts of him moving shockingly fast like the girls at the dance. I would love to tell you that they also put their talent to an artful use, but when bumping into my friend a few years 'After', only blind hatred toward me radiated through the clipped replies to my queries of her life. Racism doesn't breed creative thinking.

ALL KINDS OF HEAT

Linda and I loved every member of one of the local bands that played the dances. John and Mary's Grocery Store Band was named after the drummer's parents' old store in tiny San Antonio, the next town over. Well, Frank was off limits as Linda called permanent dibs. John played keyboard, a sweetie pie and always kind to us. Butch was the lead guitar. Even though he was a little older than the others he still showed us respect. I pretended to make out with them during each of my crushes using the back of our divan like I did with all the Beatles. Hey, I was twelve and you did too!

Linda and I had a pre dance ritual. We'd find her sister's car and while smoking a Taryton (John's choice, we noticed) we'd describe to each other what we wished we looked like. The fantasy of our outfits was important as an image booster as we were none too pretty and both fat and tall for our age. It was always the same. Linda's colors were purple and pink. I secretly lusted for that combo but took purple and yellow (the only other choice) for friendship sake. We imagined hip huggers with the wide bells and belt of the time and a matching shorty vest over a ruffled long sleeved blouse, tucked in to show off our sleek bods. A TV cartoon band would eventually copy our fabulous look (so proud!). Our hair was luxuriously long and blonde, make-up and nails perfect, unlike the preteen botch job we would apply in real life. The make-up thing didn't last too long with me. Too much crying and my budding hippiedom took care of that.

After enough convincing we'd go in and pull chairs next to one of the massive speakers, prop our feet on the stage and openly drool over them in adoration. We felt fabulous and nothing could stop us... until the inevitable slap of reality snapped us out of it. But that first breath walking through the door was exhilarating. The dance floor was in the shadows of the band lighting. The AC cranked cool air into the hot intoxication of colognes  and raging hormones. Drugs and alcohol had not yet overtaken and deadened our senses to the raw beauty of young life and every nerve took on the natural electrical charge. Fantasy still intact, confidence surged through me. Those poor boys on stage were so kind to their pudgy little groupies, always smiling and sometimes even winking at us during a certain lyric they knew would send us right over the edge. Thank you, John.

Frank had the misfortune of living only a few fields away from Linda. One afternoon we decided on a surefire plan to 'accidentally' get his attention, results being him falling in love with her. 'Surefire' turned out to be the glowing operative word. We prettied up as best we could and snuck over to his back field. The plan was to light a little fire, yell for help and Frank would come running to the rescue. Not exactly the turn of events. Within minutes of lighting a pile of completely dry grass in the completely dry field on a breezy day, over two acres were dotted with flames.

Yes, we DID spend the afternoon with Frank, but he was in no mood to fall in love with Linda. He was 19 years old and rightfully irritated with his fat little fireflies and made sure we knew it. Even so, after all the flames (and tears) were doused and it was finally safe for us to part ways, he flashed a smile my way. A few years later and well into the hippie lifestyle, we 'dated', if you could call it that. No sex as he had the more age appropriate Barbara for that, but we did our share of making out and sat together among our group of friends and such.

Back to the dances. One night, I was hanging out on the picnic tables when Jim showed up. He was tall, dark, handsome and mysterious. He hardly spoke but not from meanness or being snooty. All the girls loved him. He sat down next to me, scattering the other kids. I'd never had any kind of contact with Jim so it was a complete surprise when he asked me to be his girlfriend. He pulled out this huge gold ring with a big fat diamond (glass) in it and put it on my finger. He kissed me and left.

I didn't see him again until a week later when he asked for the ring back. Not vested in the relationship, wonder was my only reaction. I eventually learned that he had a new girlfriend every week decided solely by who was wearing the ring. I figured that after his Dad noticed his son's new carnival ring he innocently laughed out something like " Hey Boy, you could have a different girlfriend every week with that big ole' thing!"

One Saturday night found me alone outside the bowling alley smoking a cigarette. I had switched to Kools by then, pack opened from the bottom so only your own fingers touched the filter as the current trend dictated. Almost 13 now I had slimmed down, was popping out a bit and had reached my full height of 5' 6". A manboy approached, asked for a light and we struck up a conversation. After a while he suggested that we get a drink. I looked directly at him and said "I'm only twelve years old." Whenever I need a good laugh that boy's reaction does the trick.

After the move into town my weekend curfew was midnight but "NO LATER. And I want to know where you are and who you're with." And she always did. The pool room was high on the list of activities and I became quite good at it 'for a girl'. I played after school but dinner, homework and the pleasantries of our new home brought me home early. My favorite outfit for the poolroom was a pair of orange cut-offs and a black sweatshirt with the words "Sock it To Me" in neon colors on the front. Sadly, I was not out of style.

Bob also played and he showed me some helpful tips like keeping the back end of the stick down and how to figure the angles. Mother never filled our heads with silly things like 'Girls have to act this way' and 'Only boys can do that' so when I played pool I played to the best of my ability, never a thought of letting the boy win. And when the boy won that was fine and dandy too. I loved it in there. So much activity going on but it was clean and safe, unlike the rougher pool hall I would occasionally visit after Wild Child emerged.

I had pool room friends, too. Debra provided equal competition and her older brother was cute, sweet and playing even better, he helped us along like Bob did. Eventually the rumor hit my ears that Debra and her brother had had sex with each other but having already heard Mary's story it wasn't quite the shock to my young ears as one would expect. Let's play pool!

BANDANA BONDING

I connected immediately with the Hippie ideals of peace, love and understanding that were permeating the air and was permitted to be outspoken about it as believing in equality for all and general consideration for others was the norm in my family. Linda's interests were in a new boy she had met (and would marry) and we started going our separate ways. I met Helene who soon became my best pal and other kids who shared our views were easy to spot what with the particular fashion statements that went along with that movement. We started forming a tight little group. The dances no longer captivated me.

Bob and I shared a bedroom but he had won a scholarship to Dartmouth and wasn't home much so Mother let me decorate the room anyway I wanted. It being 1968, my Hippieness was in full flower power psychedelia. Everything was done in black and white; the walls, twin beds, desk, chair, all of it. I painted a Jackson Pollack type floor (I managed it sober) and set up a small table with a black satin cloth and candles forming a shrine to the giant Jimi Hendrix poster on the wall above. The black ceramic candle holder was a Menora but I was unaware of that. That it held so many candles was the attraction.

When Bob was home he slept in The Garage most of the time. Mother had wisely allowed us to take the place over as our hang-out so we could do the experimentation that accompanied our child to teen transformation within the safety of home base. We learned about sex, drugs and rock n' roll of course, but also about divorce and general loss, racism and other hatreds, love, sadness, death, jealousy, true friendship, longing, insanity, oh and puberty all within the comforting hug of a loving group of close friends and an understanding Mother nearby. But most of the time we'd just hang out and chat it up over blaring music. Plus there was my crazy dog. Everyone loved Judy.

Bob and his friends were the main contributors of the sex and drinking education in our after school curriculum. On one occasion though, as my 17 year old friend and I were hanging 'balloon' condoms for Bob and his date that evening (one of those sibling jokes that Neh-ver gets old), I remember thinking it backwards that since I was still years away from using them, I had to tell her what they were really for.

My group contributed most of the pot smoking portion of our off campus tutelage. Taking a presidential stance, it took twice several times before I inhaled and got stoned. When I finally did, it turned out that I didn't like it that much as it lasted way too long and made me laugh inappropriately and uncontrollably. I've never had a problem laughing but I do like to keep the upper hand with it.

Most of the others really enjoyed pot though so it was always around. Back in the late '60's you could get a fat ounce of killer

Jamaican or Columbian for $20.00. The few times I did smoke, it was the Jamaican, a much lighter in spirit kind of high. Once after a few hits of Columbian, I sat in a chair for hours, unable to move or even think. Why the heck would I want to do that? I was good to go with the happy buzz of a shared bottle of Ripple or Boonesfarm.

Dade City's population was about 15,000 people then and we seemed to be the only hippies so far. I might say 50 or so if all were counted but it was a smaller core group. I thought of us as a family. Claude was my boyfriend on and off for years. He pointed out that most of us had only one parent.

Claude lived with his father, a Drill sergeant and a good guy, but he wasn't around much in Claude's teens and their house became another hang out for us. There was nothing 'homey' about it as his Mother had been gone for some time. A few random chairs in the living room along with his drum kit. The walls were bare. The ever important record player was often blaring "The Court of the Crimson King". I never saw a lot of food in the fridge either. Our friend Mark found him once, almost dead and splayed out in the shower stall, glue bag in hand. He was around 13. During high school after I got sent away he lived in an abandoned Corvair in a grove for a while. He'd appear with his long red hair full of sticks and who knows what else, back stooped from sleeping in the small car and coming off of some hallucinogen, wild eyed and laughing maniacally.

Thankfully Claude was blessed with a head packed full of brains in sharp working order, an extremely pure heart and an amazing group of friends. His Dad proved to be a constant in the long run so the ocean that was roaring within him eventually calmed. He found real love which I am happy for. He's a fine man and deserves his solid ground.

I am forever discovering things not yet learned or experienced because my Mother was taken so early but she left me with a firm foundation to fall back on in unsure times. The ground I grew up walking on was rock solid and after finally learning to stand again that's my base when faced with a problem.

There were those years 'After' when my own ocean roared. Thunderous waves crashed in my head. My body laboriously trudged through life's waters and even small waves often swept me under. It was a continual search for stability. While I couldn't feel that solid ground, I knew it was out there somewhere.

Surviving those storms makes you strong in ways, but battles that size leaves scars. To survive, one often goes deep. I call it floating. Your soul/mind/spirit 'detaches' and the body feels more like protection than part of you. You find a safety way back inside that has been taken away or never existed. Those of you who have been sexually abused may know what I'm talking about. Oh, any kind of life's delightful traumas can trigger floating. You can function normally in the 'real' world, but from your new vantage point, no one can touch what really matters.

The impact that group of friends made on my life is undeniable. They were there, really there when that ocean was knocking me around and without them I would have drowned. I love them all today even though while I whole heartedly remain 'Earth Girl', (one of my nicknames) others have chosen different, sometimes darker paths.

Mark E. loomed large. His dad was a widower and owned the E & M restaurant in town, out of which Mark carved a little underground supply line. I still had dinner to come home to, but Mark sure kept Claude alive. Others as well and I believe with full knowledge of his kind father. He would come to my rescue at a very crucial point. He's the Mark I disappointed with my lack of horse riding abilities. He is a real life cowboy, after all.

Brenda had only a Mother, but unlike mine, she was not at all pleased when Brenda and I both started dating black guys. Brenda came across as shy but there was a strength in her that no one could shake. I wish I got to know her better but she wasn't around when I moved back after being freed.

James was our own personal Bob Dylan though he didn't find it the compliment I intended. I came to understand that he was our own personal James and no one else. James floated in a different way as he was a few inches above the ground all the time. Very reachable, but we all automatically looked up to him. This is the James with the saving kiss on the night of the murder.

Mitchell played a heart wrenching guitar but his shyness level had him performing with his back to the audience. My crush on him was not in the cards. He met and married another girl early on, together still. I'm happy for their solid union but at that time what mattered was to get his attention so I downed a bottle of Aspirin. I remember feeling disoriented and numb for about three days and as it left my system the whole silly business went with it. I don't

Carla, Bobby, Stewart, Mitchell, and Vicki.
I can't possibly say everything I want to say
about this picture!

even think Mitchell aware of the stunt so it was all for nothing. Thank God for the Steinle constitution!

Albert was quiet, not so sure about shy, maybe just watching and educating himself through his big blue eyes.

My friend Kathy was older and not a part of our hippie group. I would talk to her about things I couldn't

Kathy. She sent me this picture, just keeping in
touch after she'd moved out on her own. (Haha!)

share with the rest. Say two of my friends were arguing. It wasn't my business but still affected me because I loved them both. I could discuss it with Kathy safely. Everyone should have a 'remote' friend to confide in so their judgment isn't clouded. It's Kathy's Mom who tried to get visitation rights during my jail time.

There was the Peterson family from Minnesota, I believe. Bill was one of the people with me the night of the murder. Tom had confessed that he had never seen a black person in real life until moving south. It was probably similar to the first time I saw an apple tree, the red being where the orange usually was.

Bobby and Billy Stewart had an enormous intellect. Both on the quiet side, smiling and kind hearted, they spoke slowly with men's voices. Their closeness was evident by their quick glances and inside jokes like Bob and I had.

Neil was a big blond canister of sugar. He gave me a hug once in a much needed moment. If it were describable in words, that hug would be the dictionary's definition of what a hug should be and is capable of achieving.

Henry was the director and possibly the writer of a movie we made called the Izzard of Woz. I never saw the movie, so I'm assuming my pounding waves rolled in during the making of it.

BOOK BREAK

I wrote a few short stories before the book started forming and I thought I'd share one to help set the scene for this time period.

FIRST KISS

A person's first kiss is often something that is written about in little pink diaries or bragged on over a stolen six pack of beer. Neither of those treatments seemed to give my first kiss the importance it deserved...at least not to me.

I first met Helene as she got off the bus at our Junior High School, the newly built one up on the hill by the fair grounds. She was among the first batch of black kids to integrate our lily white central Florida education system. Back then, there was no mixing of the races within neighborhoods. There was a living, breathing 'across the tracks', although it had spilled over a bit on the north end near the orange juice factory. Helene lived in the spilled over portion.

I noticed her bandana headband immediately, a sure sign of a hippie in 1968. Sporting a thin leather one myself, I went right over to welcome her and we became fast friends. My Mother had not one prejudice bone in her little body so Helene was comfortable hanging out in 'The Garage' with our other hippie friends. It was a safe place away from those who got their kicks screwing with the lives of anyone different than themselves. Some got more attention than others but we all made it through. Well, almost all.

I was accepted into Helene's home life as well. Her house made me angry. It was a tiny slanted bare wood shack greedily split into a duplex. Her Mom had the bedroom, just big enough for a full sized bed. The brother slept on the couch in the living room while Helene, her twin sister Hope, and a younger sister shared a triple bunk bed on the far wall of the kitchen. The 'bath' was a round metal tub brought in from outside and the toilet was a pot that stayed out back. For this they paid (to own) $700.00 a month in 1968. Of course that wasn't the price on the original deed, but "Fees, you know Ma'am", blah, blah, blah. Still brings on the same anger today. Despite all, there was some laughter and I felt welcome.

Across the street was her Aunt Leola's 'Kitchen', another wooden shack that fed a zillion people who couldn't otherwise afford a daily meal. Walk up to the counter and for $2.00, Aunt

Leola, a small woman showing her hard life, would hand you a to go box containing a colorful landscape of whatever kind of potato or rice, vegetables, meat and bread she had cooked that day. Always delicious and there was enough food to feel the life flow back into your body.

I met most of Helene's relatives and neighbors there, including a few of the newly recruited high school football stars. Helene's cousin Arthur was destined for a pastor's life, another Arthur charmed with humor and became a lawyer. Moses was serious and caring and was later known as Dr. Baker. Being one of the few white people to enter Aunt Leola's but only a young girl, I presented no threat and was never made to feel uneasy.

There was a playground near Helene's house that for no reason acted as a neutral zone for racism. One day a bunch of us were tearing around in the dirt, sliding, swinging and spinning our little hearts out. It was dusk, a nice warm, breezy day coming to a close. I was sitting on a picnic table next to the future pastor Arthur, both of us taking a monkey bar break. He was 16 to my 12 and head to toe gorgeous. Football build, dazzling warm smile, understanding green eyes, creamy milk chocolate skin. Classic Greek God handsome all over. He radiated comfort, a calming peacefulness.

Our conversation led to him asking if I had ever kissed a black person. Well, I'd never kissed ANY person so summoning whatever sliver of 'cool' I could locate, my answer was the simple and purposely misleading "No". He then very politely asked if he could kiss me. The words "Happily Ever After" appeared in a brief flash before my young eyes, not yet aware of an appropriate image to conjure up. I'm not sure if I verbally responded, but when I turned my face to him he leaned in and gave me the most innocent kiss my lips would ever feel. 'See', he said, "there's no difference at all". "Ohhhhh, that's what he was going for", my brain quickly explained, tamping down my preteen emotions. We exchanged a knowing smile and joined in with the mix of now only dust colored kids, all unaware that they were showing the world how it should behave.

>>>>>>>>>>>>>>>>>>>>>>>>>>>>>>>>>>>>>>>

HERON SHOOTIN' HIPPIES

Dade City was football proud. The stadium up by the new Junior High received a makeover while my brother was on the team. It was probably a money issue, but it came across as a very one sided power trippy renovation. Our Pasco Pirates seating was now solid concrete with bathrooms and a concession stand underneath, its size and luxuries lording over the rickety wooden bleachers that remained the oppositions.

And we had a great team, what with the Arthurs, Moses, Greg and Andrew Pittman, Carlton and Dave all recruited from the bussed in kids. One of the Pittman brothers was featured in the year book in a (fully uniformed) Burt Reynolds Playgirl pose with a stalk of straw in his mouth. Small town country stuff. So what if he was black, he was leading our team. Integration seemed to be working.

Well, that is if you disregarded things like the 'White' and 'Colored' water fountains at the grocery stores or the popular old downtown bar with a back room for 'Coloreds'. When rebuilding in the '80's (that's the 1980's), the same plain concrete backroom was added on and for the same reason. Oddly, one black AND gay man had a spot in the front bar. And well liked, I believe…someone must have taken the time to get to know him.

I started openly dating Dave which apparently crossed the line of what was acceptable integration. Brenda was already dating Moses secretly and there were others hiding away for the same reason, but the thought of keeping such an innocent relationship a secret never occurred to me because of my Mother's open-mindedness.

The biggest reason our hand holding became so public was due to the next door neighbor on the Garage side. He was the town barber and once he zeroed in on what was happening inside our Den of Evil and Hedonism, he kept his eyes, ears and mouth WIDE open. A head of gaping holes. News spread fast that all the long hairs were in there shootin' herons and the place was "lousy with n.....s!" Attitudes quickly darkened and trouble was in the air.

When Helene and I decided to get a soda one day after school before heading home, the storm was still in its early stages. We were thirteen and had something fun and detailed to talk about and wanted a coke and the comfort of AC to do it in.

We walked into Keifer's Pharmacy and took a couple of seats at the counter. I ordered and we dove into the topic at hand. Too much time had passed with no service, so I politely reminded waitress again. More time and still no sodas. The counter was empty and the waitress was nervously wiping down every square inch of her domain. I asked again adding that we had to get home soon. She was definitely upset by something, nearly jumping out of her skin as she walked away.

The big clock above the milk shake machine said we'd been there over an hour and still no service. I made one more request trying to hide my annoyance. She stood still, eyes darting everywhere, hands fidgeting with her mop rag. I glanced over at Mr. Kiefer high up behind his pharmacy counter in time to see him nod slightly to the waitress. She served us, ripped off her apron and disappeared. We finished up, left the money plus a dime for our troubled waitress on the counter and headed home with blind innocence to the bit of history we had just contributed.

Dave. He is what all the commotion was about! A teenager with kittens!

My eyes opened wide soon after that though, as everyone started baring their teeth. At school my friend Debbie walked up to me, sneered out "You disgust me!' and spat in my face. She was one of many. Students 'accidentally' knocked hard into me and a group of senior boys pushed and shoved me up the stairs. One of those boys sat in a class across the hall, repeatedly making faces and shooting the bird. I thought it pretty funny…a senior acting so childish. Then Dave got beat up. Not funny at all. One Saturday night at the dance across the tracks, I noticed a group of girls staring at me. Judging by their expressions, they weren't thinking BFF. Fortunately, Dave rushed us to leave with his own problem trailing and I was happy to oblige. I'm surprised a burning cross never fouled my yard as a friend hiding her relationship experienced one. None of this dissuaded us, but we were not a match made in Heaven and broke up for the normal reasons any two young kids do.

I was firmly an outcast now but considering by whom it didn't matter. Our group of friends was growing with bonds kept tight. The Garage was a safe haven and my Mother knew and liked the lot of us. The barber was going out of his mind with tall tales of debauchery and devil worship, but we calmly continued to receive our guidance from the Beatle records played in reverse, sacrificing goats and casting spells over the townspeople.

FLIPSIDE

Regret is not a big part of my life because again, the Mother Show… screw up, deal with it, move on. Life puts too much weight on one's shoulders by its own doing to add in the heaviness of regret. But aside from the grief my crime wave caused, there is one other thing involving a boy. We had a great relationship; respectful, considerate, loving. And we had fun. So much fun in fact that we ended up skipping a collective six weeks in my ninth grade year. (I was Very Good at imitating Mother's signature on an excuse note.)

He had a jeep and we'd go cruisin'. We'd often end up in Zephyrhills, the land of trailer parks and retired Northerners who were done shoveling snow. We'd go into a 'For Sale' lot pretending we were married (at 13 and 16) and in need of a starter home. The sales people never followed us, the smell of money not emanating from our auras, so we'd sit in the living room and talk or sometimes have a little innocent make out session in one of the bedrooms. It was all quite romantic.

The first time we seriously kissed was movie scene romantic but I was too immature to handle it and giggled my way out of it. I still have one of the notes he gave me. The Zepplin line "Inspiration's what you are to me" framed by some of his own drawings.

To digress (again), Led Zepplin and the Allman Brothers were THE bands and both terribly important to us all. I still think they're the best in rock and when I want to get in or out of a mood, I toss in one of their CDs. The talent within those two groups is immeasurable and their songs expressed so many of our emotions. Playing as one mind, their jams flowed like a river, the instruments singing their own lyrics.

Oh yes, the regret part. I broke up with this perfect, respectful, handsome, responsible, well rounded, romantic, completely fun boy for no good reason at all. Another boy had expressed interest and I went for it, not a thought about what I was doing entered my empty head. (I was a virgin for three more years so I'm just talking about 'hanging out' here). Of course the other boy wasn't worth it at all, how could he have been? And my feelings for the first boy hadn't changed. I blatantly hurt him for what, curiosity?

I still remember vividly the day I ran into him 'After' at Ralph's butcher shop. He came in with his brothers no doubt to load up for one of their family cookouts. I said 'Hi' and even though he said it back, I sensed he would have preferred me being the hamburger behind the glass.

I remember fantasizing as I waited in line about how good it would have felt to have come in with him, holding hands and laughing, feeling protected and loved by his brothers as well, being part of their family. Perhaps his Mother and I would have become close and we could talk about the many things I was so desperately in need of discussing.

We have visited in these recent later years. He has a loving wife, children to be proud of and all the other fixins' of a happy life. I don't dwell on the 'what could have been', but I have allowed myself on more than one occasion to imagine the influences that kind of solid relationship might have had on future romances had I let it grow and be nurtured.

TRAVEL TALES

There would often be a transient or two somehow finding our little town, taking a much needed break from hitchhiking across the country. Hitchhiking was becoming the normal, even preferred mode of transportation for the free spirited. I did it all the time, alone or with Helene usually. It was safe for a while and I personally never experienced any bad rides. Oh sure, a couple of rude comments about my 'nice jiggle' and when Sherry joined us 'After' there was the suggestion of a four way with the driver. Hah! Like he could have handled THAT. Our Sherry alone would have exhausted him. After I met a girl who had been brutally raped and then a sweet boy who was later killed by his ride I never did it alone again, but at this point there was little worry.

David Dixon was one of those transients. What a crazy man! He had a broken leg that never seemed to bother him, or perhaps even appear to him as the prescribed painkillers nicely augmented his continual acid trip. He was handsome in the manner of a current friend Larry Paciello, the "Italian Stallion" as Larry modestly jokes. David was wild in his eyes and his laugh, though. Not evil, but that kind of freed wildness when you're not afraid of anything.

Since his cast extended from ankle to upper thigh, he spent a lot of time in The Garage. He brought in a reel to reel tape recorder and made long tapes that would take you on an emotional roller coaster. He was excellent at it. Every song would take you one step closer to whatever emotion he was trying to achieve. You'd find yourself going up, up, up, teetering at the top of glee, lust or love and then slowly begin the decent into a sad and lonely despair, wallowing at the bottom until you began to feel the lightening of the load as the progression of songs lifted you from your misery. Life's normal ride played out in music. I have wondered where that genius brain of his took him. I have wondered if he is still alive.

I say he wasn't evil although he told me once of a 'practical joke' he pulled on a friend. The friend had stated how much he hated the song 'Crimson and Clover' so David thought it would be hilarious to lock him in a room and repeatedly blast the song in his ears. He dosed him with acid and kept him in there for 17 hours!

Acid never excited me that much. Like pot, it was too long of a time to be out of control, but I did do it three times. My first time was on a Saturday in the little park of San Antonio, the nearby town with the big personality. Mark had set it all up. A bunch of us were to meet in the park, do acid and see where the day took us. All accounted for, Mark passed out the acid…LSD 25. This was about as high a grade as it got and it didn't take long before we were all on the same rocket heading for that happy planet up ahead. Mark decided to speak 'duck' the entire time which he excelled at and I laughed continually for the next eight or so hours. He also entertained us by imitating the engine sounds as the name of the corresponding motorcycle. For instance, Yamaha was a high pitched whine…Yaaaahh-ma-haaaah. Harley-Davidson was a low gravely rumble and so on. We all stayed in the park, gazing up at the clouds and playing on the merry-go-round with no 'freak outs' or panicking in any way.

Miraculously I remembered that I had a Mother and something called 'dinner' was often eaten with her within this hour of what some knew as 'time'. There was no way I was going to pull that off without her noticing my new spongy texture so a plan was devised.

I would enter the upright glass coffin that stood in front of the giant box of food with magic doors and summon my Mother's voice through a black box by inserting a round silvery color. I was to tell her that I was having dinner at a friend's house and would be home later…without laughing.

Mark had come up with this plan and was helping by standing outside the glass coffin and coaching me on my words…in 'duck'. Frankly, I have no idea what my Mother heard on her end but I made it home well before midnight and in hindsight I'm sure she was greatly relieved to find that my condition was not permanent.

I managed to put Mother through a few more of these nerve fraying tests before she was taken from us. Hearing about the Byron Pop Festival in Atlanta, I planned to join a few friends who were going. Unfortunately the Saturday before, someone had brought a whole bottle of liquor to the party house and I passed out for the entire night. This was a first and in the sober light of morning I realized the severity of the situation. I would have to run away for good to avoid punishment or go home and take my lumps.

The idea of running away had never crossed my mind except when I was about six and emulated a cartoon. Carrying a red bandana tied on a long stick with a Mother made PB&J/apple lunch inside, I headed out the door for adventures unknown. I went to my usual play places in full sight of her and was home in time for dinner, having completely forgotten the original plan.

The thought of running away now was equally forgettable as I was happy at home with no dreamy thoughts of what I might be missing, so off I went to receive my just desserts. Wow, she WAS upset! I was grounded for a month. I can't imagine the worry I put her through. The seconds tick by SO slowly and the mind takes you to such dark corners when you are worrying and left to wait. I get edgy when my animal pals stay away all night. I would have spiraled myself deep into the ground over a child.

NINTH GRADE?

As in elementary school, the subject of my classes taught me far less than the life that was happening within them. I dropped my Math Theory class after the teacher couldn't give me an answer when asked where I would use such information. He could have said anything, especially "Shut up and you might find out", and I would have stayed, but his shoulders just drooped as he said "Probably never".

Biology also went by the wayside when I steadfastly refused to dissect a living frog. I do remember a class I had with my pal Suzanne DeRosier, but that's only because we laughed all the time.

The subject escapes me. Geography was the class where the senior boy sneered and gave me the finger from across the hall. Our teacher was Albino and occasionally mixed up some map colors. We paid closer attention and because of that some of the lessons actually stuck.

Social Studies. Half way through the year, our teachers' son killed himself. Thomas Earl was a very popular kid, handsome, funny, the whole nine yards. The story I heard was that he was diabetic and felt he was a burden to the family and left a note to that effect. Shot himself with a rifle. His Mother went nuts for a while as expected and the main hall at school seemed much darker and quieter. I didn't know him as he was two grades ahead, but my heart went out to his girlfriend. We'd had a few conversations but I wasn't sure where she stood on my new 'social status', so I cowered in the background and offered her no comfort.

Ninth grade was over and summer was on. It was play time! We weren't 'Driven by the Devil' as the rumors portrayed. A lot of driving was done but that was for scenery changes. We often went swimming in Clear Lake, the nearby Peterson house supplying forgotten towels. Of course the music was so important, locking into our memories for later emotional stirrings.

Some of us had jobs or held bigger responsibilities at home, but we still got together. The Izzard of Woz was in the making. Pot and alcohol were used but not as a way of life, and although some acid was dropped on occasion, needles were nowhere to be seen. In general there was a lot of laughing, delving into the new wave of beliefs and a tremendous closeness between us all.

And somewhere, someone was deciding that my Mother needed to die.

SECTION FOUR

JULY 18, 1970

It was Saturday night and a group of us were going out looking for some fun. We were not a criminally minded bunch so it was suggested that we go dancing at The Cow Palace, a bar deep on the other side of the tracks.

The place was huge and jam packed, live music keeping everyone moving. We were the only white folks... all bell bottoms and hair.... along with Helene in obvious hippie garb as well. No one paid us any mind other than a quick glance or a smile. I'd like to have seen that happen in reverse, but no way...not in those days.

Even though we were clearly under age, the bartender took our order. Our all white police force never came back this far into the black neighborhood. The attitude was "If they stay back there where they belong, who cares if they kill each other". I think it was more out of fear. I felt no reason for that or saw any violence, just people having fun on a Saturday night dancing to one smokin' band.

The drinking laws were laughably lax back then. A bar in the North End called the Ranch House had a drive up window. So did that newly built one in the middle of town. You could pull up like a fast food place and ice, cups and mixer would accompany your bottle and a smile would merrily send you on your way...la-la-la-la-la!

We stayed at The Cow Palace for a few drinks, but never made it to the dance floor, deciding it was too crowded. Next stop was a place called "The Moon", a clearing in the middle of an orange grove where the Moon hung bright, a safe place to gather. After that four of us decided to cap off the night in a little park on Meridian Ave., the main cross street in town. It was a cozy tree filled green division between the shops and the truly rich section of town. Stately old Plantation style homes with massive ferns adorning columned porches dotted the street beside more modern architecture like that intriguing one story Asian style.

Dade City's money mainly came from cattle and orange groves. Well, I mean to say that the percentage of millionaires was high for such a small town. That certainly didn't translate into the whole town being rich.

It was nearing midnight so my pals dropped me at home and headed to the Royal Castle four blocks away. It was the first fast food place in town and its bright lights attracted the kids like moths. It had become the custom of the nightlife to inch around the circular drive, letting the kids inside get as good a look at you as you were getting of them.

Kicking off my shoes, I noticed all the lights were out except in the empty living room where I was standing. The TV was talking loudly to no one. I called out to Mother, but no answer. My muscles stiffened but I stuck my head in the dark kitchen doorway. She was lying motionless on the floor with a blanket under her, her pants pulled down to her ankles but the red checkered dress that she liked to wear was still on and in proper place. She was unconscious, at the very least. A sharp clap of thunder boomed in my head and terror filled my veins. My breath was gone. Was someone still …? Two yellow flowered cups and saucers sat in conversation setting on the kitchen table. Our fancy ones. The chair next to Mother was knocked on its side. My eyes went left into my moonlit bedroom. The window to the back yard was wide open and the evenings' rejected outfit left on the bed was gone. Who drank from that second cup?

I bolted out the front door for the Royal Castle. My bare feet flew over the sidewalk and I met my friends just as they were pulling around the back. Screaming "My Mother's Been Raped!" I jumped into the car.

The next thing I remember was facing my friend James. We were sitting on the hoods of cars that were nosed up to each other. Lieutenant Berger, the dad of a classmate, was asking questions. I could feel my answers vibrate in my throat, but the noise in my head cancelled out the sound. The place was crawling with police and flashing lights. People were going in and out of our house. People were everywhere.

It seemed like forever or seconds had passed. Lt. Berger was writing in his notepad. I stuttered out "Is she d-dead?" He gave a look as if I were from Zertron and quietly whispered "Yes".

Whoooooosssshhh! Suddenly I was above everyone and floating upward into the quiet. In hindsight, I might suggest that there wasn't a place deep enough inside to escape so I had to go 'out'. My survival instinct must have kicked in because it wasn't long before I was back on the car's hood.

I found myself hugging and kissing James. Lt. Berger's lip rose with disapproval. What was his problem? He had just told me my Mother was dead. Murdered! He would finish up his notes and go back to his cozy little home with his pretty blonde wife and daughters. I was trying to find some reality and stay on the planet! James and I locked eyes for hours or a minute sharing the horror and fear, the sadness to come.

More blanks and blurred time. A burst of reality found me at the police station in a ridiculously bright room. I was alone sitting on a metal chair by a metal table with a ticking clock on the wall. Nothing else in the room. Somehow I had different clothes on. A camera came through the door, flashed its blinding bulb several times, then the smiling human holding it entered and asked if he could take some pictures for the St. Pete Times. You had reddish brown hair, black rim glasses, I remember your face exactly and my intense hatred of you has deepened into solid disrespect. I angrily said 'No', he smiled again and backed out. The pictures he took were printed along with a story which I'm told 'reported' that the perpetrator must have been "a n....r or some kid hopped up on drugs". They forgot to list 'racist' as a possibility.

I sat stump like and numb on the metal chair, the thunder gone for now. Our blessed minds have many powerful ways to shield us from the pain this life can inflict. Mine had simply shut down. Nothing. No thoughts.

A man entered the room with a slide show. Some of you may remember them. With a click a picture from a storage wheel pops up on a white screen. Classrooms shared them so they were kept in the projection room, a real treat to be picked for retrieval and you'd return with several outlandish excuses as to why it took so long.

The man setting up the screen said nothing to me, not even a glance at my face. He connected my arm to a machine. What's that do? He never explained. The slide show began; one bloody blade after another. Well, my mind was awake now! Click. "Have you ever seen this turkey carver?" Click. "Have you ever seen this bejeweled letter opener?" Click. "Have you ever seen this hatchet?" Of course I'd never seen any of these gruesome things and repeatedly said so. Why was he showing me such horrific pictures? The machine remained calm. The machinelike operator packed up and rolled out of the room.

The clock ticked. No water, comfort or kindness offered whatsoever, just the metal chair in the sterile neon room. The sun peeked in around the closed louvered shades. I remember thinking that I should have been tired. I felt nothing. A little cold maybe. Around midmorning a woman came in to say she was taking me somewhere to wait until my Aunt Dolores and Uncle Frank arrived from their home outside of Atlanta. They were driving so it would be a while.

The house I was to wait in was only a short walk from my cousins' old house on 3rd Street. The house where I heard my aunt's rich laugh, Frank's cornball jokes, where Dolores' Mother palmed us $5.00 every holiday. I learned to sew there, saw gigantic grasshoppers, made forts, sucked nectar from red Hibiscus flowers and joyously played with my cousins and neighbor kids. Now it seemed so out of reach, so distant. Or rather, I was.

Handing me off to a large woman wearing various blooming flower patterns, my delivery woman slipped out the door with an insincere smile. I was ushered to a bedroom just off the kitchen. Two triple bunks were being used. All occupants faced the wall, some slept, some quietly cried. I took the empty bottom bunk and was told breakfast would be ready soon. I was given nothing, not even a toothbrush, so I lay down in my clothes, pretty rank now from fear sweat, and stared at the bowing springs above me. Eventually a friendly girl with long brown hair sat up in the bunk across from me. She had been there before and began kindly filling me in on possible things to expect. I found it hard to follow as I'd never heard most of the courtroom jargon and other legalese she was so casually using.

'Breakfast' was shoveled up. It was an inane amount of food, even considering my hearty appetite. A copious mound of grits and collards, slabs of bacon, ham AND sausage, three sunny side ups with two giant biscuits to mop it all up. Massive but edible until I watched with revulsion as the human flower garden ladled pork grease over everything right before placing it in front of me. (I'm not that kind of Southern) "Eat up now, you need your strength", she bloomed.

A middle-aged man came skipping down the hall, flopped across an easy chair and giggled as he read the Sunday funnies, kicking his feet back and forth like the little kid he was inside. The brown haired girl sat down and after receiving a similar plate of food, she mouthed the relieving words that eating a small portion would make the woman happy. Scraping off the congealing layer of fat from an egg, I collected an ingestible bite.

As I raised the fork to my mouth, the radio announcer began describing in full gory detail the murder of my Mother. Apparently there was no rape involved, just the insane and desperate violence of her killing. Her jaw had been broken with a hard left hook that had knocked her out. I thank God every day for sparing my Mother of what was next to come. Her throat had been cut almost all the way through. The image burned forever into my brain from the night before has her chin resting on her chest like Jack Nicholsons' death scene in "Easy Rider". That explained why.

The announcer blandly read out the fact that there were a total of 57 stab wounds from head to toe. It was someone's job to count them. The blanket I saw her lying on in the dark was actually her own blood. Perhaps the lifeless cuts were less visible in the dark, covered by her dress, or just erased by the mercy of the mind, but they are not included in the image I carry. No wonder Lt. Berger had such a shocked reaction when I asked if she was dead.

The radio squawked on with more grisly details. The brown haired girl's face was chalk white as she lowered my paralyzed hand to the food trough in front of me. The man reading the funnies giggled incessantly while a huge grinning sunflower was prodding a statue to eat. The whisper of a young girl was counting holes in the ceiling tiles. Fellini would have approved this scene.

Bob was driving home with his friend Rocky after checking out a few colleges upstate. He and I were listening to that same radio announcement. With no prior knowledge of her death as I had, the news and all the gore was dumped on him at once. While he was driving and hours away. Perhaps part of him floated away forever right then.

Back at the boarding house, my body plodded its way back to the cot and resumed its position staring at the bedsprings above. Sleep finally overtook, but too soon my relatives arrived and I awoke with a hard smack of reality. Walking toward my Aunt and Uncle, I could see the strain on their faces. Dolores gave me a big hug and nervously stated "Well, someone needs a shower." What DOES someone say under those circumstances? 'How are you?' 'Are you okay?' Acceptable and caring questions…but don't expect a viable answer. One is not aware of themselves in the normal ways during such traumatic duress.

They had rented a few rooms for us as Aunt Poo-Poo Head and Uncle Jimmy were flying in to help sort things out. The motel was on the main drag (Hwy 301) through town and right across from the A&P where Mother and I bought groceries. It now radiated a surreal aura, my vision skewed from my safe position of deep retreat inside my body. I don't remember ever talking to or being talked to by any of the adults during that time. Charlie Brown's creator Charles Shulz depicted that kids view perfectly, just bodies wahw, wahw, wahwing from above.

Bob, being of age, was ignored until decisions were made and was expected to remain living in the house where a few days earlier his Mother had been brutally murdered.

One morning my friends came over to check in on me. We stood out front by the pool in full view for all to see. There were maybe ten of us and we huddled close together. I felt a realness that had been missing since the murder. (Several days had lapsed, not sure how many). The conversation was light, even a little harmless joking about nothing in particular…laughter being the best medicine. We were hardly laughing anyway, a few awkward muffled chuckles at best. They were all so comforting and dealing with such a horrible situation, were simply trying to bring some joy for me to hold on to.

Aunt Poo-Poo Head saw me with a trace of a smile on my face and lost her mind, my 'indifference' unacceptable after such a tragedy. (I was told this later.) Never bothering to speak to me directly, they packed their bags and left. I have never seen them again.

WHAT I DID SEE OF THEM

Uncle Jimmy owned several seats on the New York Stock Exchange and had an arkload of money, but I have become appreciative of their absence in my life despite any monetary dividend I may have eventually received. They came to visit only once back in Orange Grove Villa when I was maybe seven. Uncle Jimmy never got off the phone. He positioned himself in the front yard lawn chair with a continual drink at his side, our phone cord stretched to the limit through the kitchen window. He never looked at or spoke to me. We all went to dinner one night at the famed Columbia Restaurant in Ybor City, the Spanish section of Tampa. The kids were at the opposite end of the long table, completely ignored. He was bald, overweight and red faced, in his forties but looked decades older. It wouldn't be a surprise if an early heart attack came knocking.

The second of the two visits to them happened when I was ten. Uncle Jimmy, Aunt Poo-Poo Head and their lawyer son Terry had rented a cottage in Manasquan, N.J. on the beach and invited us up for a week. Astronaut Buzz Aldren was in the next cottage and had a Xeroxed copy sent over when asked for his autograph. I thought it was silly even then but Uncle Jimmy was so proud of it that he had it framed, totally missing the point of receiving a hand written autograph in person. No doubt they missed many points concerning the human side of life, all that money blocking their view.

TWO QUICK UNRELATED STORIES in MANASQUAN

Bob and I were out body surfing on our rafts when the perfect wave came up. Bob caught it like a pro and made it all the way into shore. I missed it and dog paddled frantically under a film of water as each tiny wave took my raft maddeningly inches away from my fingertips. I finally caught it, dragged myself up and floated like the dead seal I felt like, catching glimpses of the lifeguard sitting lifeless high up in his chair behind sunglasses, probably asleep. Bob, already searching the water, brought me in. My Hero!

I befriended a girl my age on the beach and was visiting in her nearby cottage, one large room with a curtain separating the parents' bedroom. We were watching cartoons on the sofa that backed the curtain and I could hear the parents talking quietly behind me. This caught my interest as I was not used to hearing private conversations like that at home. I noticed a slight break in the curtain and turned to peek through. They were close on the same bed, whispering. I was totally engrossed when all of a sudden the husband turned his head and looked directly into my peering eye. I jumped out of my skin, grabbed it and ran out the door never to return and never to spy again.

I went back to Georgia with my Aunt and Uncle. Bob was simply left to fend for himself. I only got to see him at the funeral. What were those crazy adults thinking? We needed each other so badly. We were best friends aside from being brother and sister and our Mother had just been murdered! We were never even told where she was buried. But being 18 and 'of age', he was left to deal with it all on his own.

JONESBORO-ROUND 1

My next 'home' was a modern split level in a newly built suburb in Jonesboro outside of Atlanta. I had my own room but was so lost that nothing mattered. The move must have been some factory recruitment thing as the family to the left was also from Dade City as well as several other neighbors sprinkled about. The son next door was three years older than me, a big difference in high school, and was barely a casual acquaintance but he was a person I knew 'Before', so I started visiting him to possibly locate some sort of ground under my feet. He was nice to me and there was no hint of romance from either side, just the big brother conversation I was so longed for. Frank and Dolores thought it was inappropriate for a 14 year old girl to be socializing with a 17 year old boy so I wasn't allowed to see him. A quick note; try to find out WHY your kids are doing what they're doing...

So instead of finding some ground, when I started tenth grade and was approached by a pimply faced bleached blonde girl who offered me a big pink pill, I said "Sure, why not?" It did nothing. None of the pills she gave me did anything and she wasn't even selling them. Not sure what her deal was, but I never got to find out as a few weeks into the school year I got called down to Dade City for more questioning. Frank and I drove down together. I love my uncle dearly, but he was one crazy driver. Did whatever he wanted to do on the road.

We were slowly zig-zagging Southbound on Interstate 75, him enjoying his distractions, me facing the passenger window trying to keep calm, when we passed a car that had crashed into the bridge abutment. The car had bounced back with the front end toward the highway. The drivers' broken face was pushed up against the windshield, his black rimmed glasses cracked and skewed, his left arm raised and bent in too many places. My apologies for sounding selfish, but this was not something I needed to see so soon after finding my own Mother's body. We kept driving, my uncle unfocused on something else and within a few minutes I heard sirens. Okay he's being taken care of, let's try to erase this from the mind.

MARK'S MAGIC BUS

The next few days are a little blurry. I don't remember being with my uncle at all while we were in Dade City. I never was called in for more questioning, something I'm sure Frank finagled. I was finally with Bob at our house. Bob had expressed some of his grief by painting the walls in the living room flat black, keeping the curtains closed and lights off most of the time. There was never a lack of alcohol and two of his friends had moved in, taking over my room and the sofa.

One night, I heard Dennis tell Bob he wanted to 'talk' to me and Bob, having accomplished his goal of numbness, said 'Fine' and stumbled off to pass out. Dennis came out of my room toward me, penis in hand and a slobbery look on his face. Fortunately, I had noticed the car keys on the server by the front door. I dove passed him, grabbed the keys, jumped in the car and got safely away. Thanks for the early driving lessons, big brother!

It was after midnight and I didn't want to wake any adults. My friend Billy was still living at home but since he was a senior his parents let him take over a separate little building off to the side. Their house was maybe ten miles away and down a long dirt road in between an orange grove and some woods. That seemed safe enough. Dashing the headlights, I pulled in and knocked lightly on the door. Poor Billy, he was so groggy and confused as he tried to listen to this hyped up 14 year old babble on about escaping forced sex and needing somewhere to stay. He was fumbling around for something helpful to do or say, but I could tell a place for me there was not an option. I removed his problem by leaving.

I thought of the old school bus Mark had parked in their small back yard behind his house and was fixing up as another hang out... like The Garage and Claude's place. Mark's own Mother had died not long before. He and his brother and father now lived independent lives, not unloving but more as three men, not under father/son rules. It ruffled no feathers when I knocked on the door in the middle of the night. Without hesitation Mark set me up with some bedding and food and told me that I was "completely safe and not to worry". In the time that followed my Mother's murder up to that night I hadn't felt the least bit safe but that seemed to go unnoticed. The weight his words lifted that night was enormous. I slept soundly in that magic bus and have always had a treasured love for Mr. Mark Edenfield.

NOTHING PLEASANT HERE

While Frank and I were in Florida, Dolores decided to go through my things looking for clues to help her connect with me. Her boy children gave her plenty to contend with, but a budding teenage girl and with my specific attached problem? I understood that even then and never bore any ill will toward her for doing so. Considering what she unearthed, I actually felt sorry for her.

You see, Bob and I were hatching my escape. He and two of his friends would come up on motorcycles, steal me away, and ride off into the sunset. In Georgia, it was (is?) legal for a 14 year old to marry without adult consent, so I was to get hitched to handsome Ricky Lombardo, making me a wife rather than a kidnap victim. I had a letter in the works asking Brenda if she would play along with the story that I was visiting her for the weekend so as to give us a big head start on the road when that call for more questioning came in from Dade City, putting the plan on hold.

My Aunt found the letter and phoned Frank right away. The worst part of this whole episode was the unrelated venting I'd included in the letter. Do you remember when you and your friends first discovered curse words? It was important to say the filthiest things you could come up with mainly to make each other laugh, right? In the town of Jonesboro, Ga. the phrase "He/she/you suck big blue hairy donkey dicks" had somehow become THE PHRASE to use. In my letter, I wrote that my Aunt and Uncle did just that. Of course, I barely even thought about what those words meant, it was just the trending phrase deemed appropriate for venting about a discomforting situation. However, my poor Aunt being unaware of that side of it, no doubt took it literally. Her mind must have temporarily flattened. I am SO, SO sorry, Dolores!

She never told Frank about that particular sparkle in the letter, but she did convey my unhappiness and they decided that the court system in Dade City should take over my custody. They had moved to

Jonesboro before my Civil Rights activities, or as some called it, my N.....-lovin' hippie s..t, had become public and had no idea it was the enemy they were delivering me to.

FIVE WEEKS

The presiding judge was a wicked little racist who made no secret of his intentions to get rid of me one way or another. Saying he was going to make some calls about temporary placement, I was to sit quietly in his outer office. I could clearly hear him agreeing with the refusal by Patty and Tex, my Mother's close friends, empathizing that he didn't expect them to take in 'someone like me'. I also heard him dismiss Mrs. Gilmore who called graciously offering her help, her daughter Leslie being a friend. He then had someone take me to what was to be my next 'home'… a jail cell.

The floor plan of the jail had a main hall down the middle with solid cell doors on either side. A smaller hall ran between the back of the cell, the side with the bars, and the outside wall where the jalousie windows were. This allowed for natural light and a view of the real world without the prisoner being able to reach the handle. My window was permanently closed.

I was not let out once in the five weeks I was held and my only non-incarcerated visitor was a spineless little fool who called himself my 'Aftercare' counselor. Had I thought to dissect the word 'aftercare', I might have asked him "After what?" But I did not and he offered no explanation. He offered nothing of use at all.

During the first three weeks, several girls came and went for a few days at a time, one being all the way from Yreka, Ca. We would have been friends. A little wild child with Orphan Annie hair stayed for almost a week, telling me all sorts of things she'd done and sounding very worldly for her 13 years. She was one of those fearless people. Took it all on and caused a good portion of it herself.

She left and I was alone for about a week, except for the one night when a serial killer on route to a maximum security prison was placed next to my cell. He had found a little piece of mirror on the top crossbar and amused himself while looking into my cell through the bars. I tried to get out of his view, but there was nowhere to go. Thank God he was taken away the next day.

A nice looking trustee maybe 20 years old would occasionally risk getting caught in the evening to slip an extra PBJ (the weekday dinner) through the food slot. He was on his way to becoming a comedian and would practice his routine for me from behind the little glass window in the door. He was a bright spot.

In the fifth week, wild child returned, confessing that she had broken into someone's home and had purposely gotten caught so she could be with me again. I thought that was stupid but kept it to myself. She never tried to touch me, it wasn't like that. She felt comfortable around me...safe maybe. She knew some crazy stuff and was happy to demonstrate some of it, like how she could make her hoo-hah 'fart' by hanging upside down off the upper bunk and doing whatever it took to make it happen. Perhaps the North End biker girl got her start this way. Despite our differences, we did laugh a lot and I felt pretty comfortable around her as well.

Back to my week alone. A broken corner of one of the closed jalousie panes in my window had fallen out and I was peeking out to grasp some of the outside world. Sent by God or my Mother, Helene was walking along the road that ran behind the jail yard and I began screaming her name. THAT AND ONLY THAT is how anyone learned where I was. The little racist judge may have planned to have me die in there. Helene spread the word and immediately Kathy's Mother and Bob set about to see me. Kathy's Mother was told only relatives could visit. Bob was told only people over 21 could visit. Finally somewhere in the next two weeks, one of them pushed hard enough to get clearance for a visit on a Sunday, the only visitor's day. (Side note...instead of the usual slop, on visitor's day for lunch we got fried chicken, real mashed potatoes and a salad. Did Edna Hoster work in a prison at some point? Maybe have an affair with or raped by a guard?) About a half an hour before visiting hours, I was whisked away and driven to a girls' school in Ocala.

All of the actions the judge and his accomplices carried out toward me were illegal, of course.

THE ALICE D. MAC PHEARSON SCHOOL for GIRLS

My 'chauffeur' pulled into the junior campus of a reform school. The uninterested police officer freed me from my back seat cage and escorted me to the receiving area of my next new 'home'. Immediately, I sensed a difference in attitude.

The receptionist was warm and welcoming without a trace of judgment. I would come to treasure our visits and had many as the receiving area was attached to my assigned cottage. In her midtwenties and well beyond pretty, she wore stylish dresses that spoke without gossip of her womanly body. She was mad, mad, madly in love and engaged to her Knight in Shining Armor who was on a Denzelian level concerning looks as well as grace. He would send random flowers or notes to her desk that would send her soaring and her uncontained joy was eagerly mopped up by whoever was lucky enough to be around her.

My counselor, a sweetie pie named Ms. Kennedy, stated right out of the gate that I should never have been sent up and while I was not to be treated as special, she was aware that the trouble causing misfit described in my file was not accurate. Alright! A little balance and understanding.

The rule has since changed, but back then a minimum six month stay was required for release and Ms. Kennedy assured me I would have to stay no longer. That is, if I behaved. The system mimicked high school in a way; one earned their way up from freshman to senior but also needed the approval of the therapy group we attended each day after school.

A two week orientation period began with a shower overseen by an older woman far too interested in the makings of a young girl's body. Two at a time in separate stalls open in the front. Debra Teague shared my time slot. While I quietly endured the woman's creepy stares Debra, a snooty socialite type, screamed "What the Hell you lookin' at?" making the woman turn away in embarrassment at being caught. I don't usually care for snooty socialite types, but Debra had a place in my heart after that.

There were several cottages on the campus, each housing 16 girls. Most had four bedrooms, mine had two. The maximum age was 14 so the majority of these girls weren't completely destroyed yet. Runaways (often running from horrible things) were common, school skippers, one 13 year old prostitute who was born an adult, some thieves and fighters, but in general they were just regular girls. We got along amazingly well.

In the therapy group, a white board listed problematic behaviors and we were to claim the ones that we connected with and try to figure out what brought them on. Running away, fighting and other anger issues, drugs, drinking, sex, authority (lack of respect for), lying, bullying, stealing and cheating were already being discussed when I joined in. Murdered Mother in a Racist Run Town was not in the mix, so Ms. Kennedy assigned 'Authority' as my issue. I agreed that I probably didn't have much respect for certain authority figures I had recently encountered.

Sex was a BIG subject and I naively let it be known that I was a virgin. Virginity among these girls was steak tartar rare and it soon spread all over campus. One of the few true lesbians on campus made it known that she was going to break me in with a coke bottle. (What was the deal with coke bottles in your hoo-hah?) Anyway, she never did and I don't think she even knew who I was, but the fear of it stayed in the back of my mind.

I say 'true' lesbian as it was the trend to pal up, hold hands and perform other PDA's when you were outside of your own cottage. It probably got started for safety sake through the buddy system, but it had grown to become more of a social trend at this point.

Another statement was to wear the Government Issue state bucks with dignity. (Remember the bus trip to Tampa?) These were reddish brown leather oxford lace up shoes that no clothes conscious person would be caught dead in out in the 'real' world. It must have been The Coolest Girl on Campus that got this fashion going because they were U-G-L-Y! But here now, they were proudly worn with rolled up jeans and white socks, dresses of all lengths, shorts, sometimes with jammies in the evening. A power play to the ego was forced on these girls and they took control of it, reversing the dynamic. A small victory, but even tiny wins elevate the spirit.

Fortunately another hippie girl named Dyan shared my cottage so we did the hand holding thing and were never bothered. We were also the only two on the entire campus that could do our schoolwork from high school level books. Everyone else labored through the color coded S.R.A. kits introduced in second or third grade in public schools. Our teacher was so impressed with our 'intelligence', that when we finished our six months and released, he bumped both of us up to 11th grade graduates, skipping through two years. The reality of it was that he taught us nothing, having us work off of each other instead and only required the minimum from us. Thanks.

WHAT THE...?

This may interest some of you. Soon after settling in, I was in the library on a low stool searching the bottom row. I noticed someone standing next to me pulling out a book from a higher shelf. It's my nature to acknowledge someone's presence, but before fully turning my head the person faded. I did get a peripheral side image. It was me...in my seventh grade graduation dress (lime green with big white polka dots, hard to miss). I've tossed this around many times trying to figure out what the heck that was all about. What was I being shown? To rely on myself? Don't forget the 'Before'?. The book I was looking for was a few rows up (haha)? I don't know, but it happened and my mind stays more open because of it.

A BIG LITTLE THING

Butch Obert, the guitarist in that local band I loved, sent me a comfort note. I rarely saw him off stage which made it a surprise and quite special. When signing his name, he made some little error. Above the signature, he wrote "Has trouble spelling own name". Considering how lost I was, his casual and humorous admission to a mistake meant the world to me. Here he was, implying that I was a normal human being capable of equally relating to another. Standing in the sterile hallway of my new 'home', a tiny light beckoned in the darkness.

ARMCHAIR PSYCHIATRY SCHOOL

Despite the lack of traditional schooling, the experience was enormously educational, especially those after school group sessions. Each meeting the 16 of us gathered in the living room to openly discuss someone's problem. Ms. Kennedy was present but only as a gentle guide to keep us on track. More often than not, the spotlighted one would sob out the awful truths that sparked their unacceptable actions. Other girls would tear up with empathy. No one laughed or taunted inappropriately. Hugs were allowed and generously given. I couldn't help seeing the relief of a housemate as she shared the painful story of her raging father, psychotic Mother or just plain lack of food or care of any kind. As a result, it's easy to talk about my issues with a willing ear. Well, it eventually became easy.

My brother received absolutely no help in dealing with Mother's murder or any of the problems stemming from it.

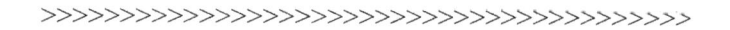

Hahahahahahaha!

On the weekends this room where we routinely splayed ourselves turned back into being 'just' a living room. Several of us would gather to watch TV and groom ourselves sharing the girlie products the rare functioning parent sent from home. I've always had long hair (aside from the chop-chop in third grade) and someone offered to plat it up like other girls did. It took hours and the next day after taking the braids out, I had a massive Afro that hung half way down my back. It straightened with washing so it became a source of entertainment for two or three girls to work together at it. These evenings in the living room were peaceful, giving a group of floating strangers some real down to Earth closeness with one another, something many of them had never experienced.

>>>>>>>>>>>>>>>>>>>>>>>>>>>>>>>>>>>>>>

As I said, sex (and sex adjacent stuff) was a big focus and everyone had at least some experience. Two of my roommates made it their goal to shock me…virgin me. As I entered the room, Maxine and Pam grabbed Brenda, ripped off her panties and spread her legs. Seeing her embarrassment, I gave the girls a bored look and walked passed emotionless. Their antics were futile without the proper reaction, so they gave up. I would remember that!

After lights out most of the girls would lie on their backs, knees up. I never gave it a thought until one night the little prostitute whispered that she had stolen a pickle jar from the kitchen and began passing them out. Okay then, pillow over my ears and Good Night, Ladies.

One morning out at the clothes line, Meatball, her nickname earned by the two giant round 'Meatballs' on her otherwise tiny frame, asked if I would ever marry a girl. After some thought my 14 year old self answered that I would probably marry a dog if I found myself in love with one. I have never married but apparently the lack of options is not the reason.

This was the general level of conversation carried on by our group of 11-14 year old girls. The subject matter was elephant weight. Breezy chatter might include whether a parent would be released for a birthday visit, what relative overdosed or voicing the hope that the next foster parents weren't abusive. A chat up might start by reviewing what came out in a group session or what someone wanted to reveal in a future one. It was raw and real. Who had the coolest Barbie clothes never came up. Getting hit in the face with a Barbie a mother angrily grabbed off the store shelf would more likely be the topic.

I don't want to mislead you, there was a lot of laughter but a good portion was done as a healing mechanism. I've already confessed to being born with a comedian's take on things. It was in this place where I developed the habit of poking the tender center with the humor stick. I have altered a few long and solid friendships by not realizing what truths a person can and cannot handle. It hurts me to see a friend suffer in silence from a painful memory or to ignore a current problem rather than slap its face and take control of it. I forget that I was taught to do this early in life when I barely knew I was learning it. I can't stand having an emotional thorn in my side, tossing and turning at night, miserable and useless thoughts endlessly rolling around in my head. I don't want anyone else to endure that either. Let's talk about it, shred it and toss it in the trash. Some people aren't capable of being that direct. I am Still learning how to speak to someone who has obviously built a barrier wall in front of their pain. Sometimes when that wall cracks a bit, I tend to forget that what is exposed behind it is private property and I should wait to be invited in. I have to remind myself to be a more patient friend and see what joys and relief might come from that on its own.

VISITS

Dolores, Frank and the boys came up for a visit once and Dolores had lost all of her extra weight. Weight Watcher's coupled with intense stress made that magic happen. She was sporting a new navy pant suit and was much taller than I had ever noticed. This was the first time I had seen her since she found my horrible note so the visit started out stiff and uncomfortable, but our joy in seeing each other quickly relaxed us and with lots of hugging and laughing that whole business was put behind us. I loved her so much.

My junior level allowed for a two hour off campus visit to a public place that was probably monitored. Bob did his best and his best was great. He packed his van with as many of my pals that would fit and dropped them off at the appointed fast food place to wait while he signed me out. Oh my God was that a healing visit! This time there was hearty laughing right out loud for all to see and hear without scorn and abandonment. So many of my 'family' showed up having written poems, letters, drawn cartoons and other symbols of love that I have saved to this day. The emptiness in my soul was being filled as a cold body warms from a winter soup.

After earning my senior status, I was allowed to go home for the weekend. Hhhhmmm, home. Now where was that? This curiosity on the school's part never occurred to me until writing this. Bob must have proven trustworthy again and was allowed to sign me out. Mark's bus fit the bill once more.

There was a big party going on in someone's barn that weekend and unbeknownst to me something was put in my cup which had a mild speedy effect. Poor Claude drove me 'home' and we sat outside in his big truck waiting for Mark to arrive, me babbling away. I finally noticed that he had fallen asleep. The sting of actually boring someone to dreamland was minimalized by my extra mental energy.

It was a windy night and across the street was a tall stand of woods. I didn't want to wake Claude so I entertained my mind by staring unfocused at the swaying trees. It wasn't long before shapes began forming within the branches. I found this delightful and allowed my mind to open wide and flow where ever it wanted. The moon and streetlights filtering through added light and shading like a painting and the breeze brought in movement and life. After a while fully formed people were interacting. At one point a group of trees took the shape of a grizzled old man with a beard, his cap pulled down close to his eyes. He looked straight at me while aiming a wide gun barrel at my face.

I was immediately jolted back to reality, a little shaken but excited about what I had stumbled upon. I tried the trick back on campus using the wavy bathroom tiles as the canvas and it worked! Relaxing my eyes and mind, lifelike movement began to form. Who needs drugs? Our brain is one big tab of acid when we open up to it.

It happened again by accident the very next year while waiting for my roommate Lynn. She needed to pay a visit to an ailing family friend and said she'd be about 15 minutes. She was gone for hours. I was left standing in front of an empty storefront with bare lots on either side. There was nothing I could do but wait…and wait…and wait. Boredom can be a key factor to this strange but fascinating activity. Shut down those tedious, worrisome thoughts and fly! When Lynn finally walked up, I was lying on the sidewalk fully engaged in some imaginary scenario like I used to do as a kid in the grass.

Yes, I do realize that after a certain age lying on a public sidewalk waving my hands at nothing would appear that I had lost my mind.

Those wavy tiles I mentioned were in the private bathroom of the senior's room I shared with a girl named Shirley who had earned the same privileges. She was tall and skinny with the huge brown eyes of someone constantly startled. We had different schedules during the day but at night in our beds, she would tell me wild stories about the spirits who occasionally took over her body. They temporarily controlled her Grandmother and several other relatives as well. She lived way out in the country and her descriptions had me visualizing a ramshackle cottage in a dark forest, a huge iron pot outside bubbling up something thick and green.

One night at the Canteen, the stark cement block rectangle that served as a dance hall for those deemed deserving, Shirley fell on the floor and began screaming "The Spirits got me, the Spirits got me!" She was kicking and shaking, eyes bulging, her own hands at her throat. (Oh my God, she's been telling me the truth?) One of the chaperones rushed over and stuck her finger in Shirley's mouth, calling out for someone to get the nurse. It was over quickly, Shirley was taken care of and I learned about Epilepsy. Shirley never did though and continued to tell me tales of her family and the spirits that governed them. I think about her occasionally and what kind of life she's living. It is a reality to her that spirits use her body from time to time and she watches as they pass through other family members. They enter, they leave, and life goes on. They took no medicine and the grandmother lived at least long enough to become a grandmother.

I repeat, I may not have come away with much in the way of traditional schooling, but I certainly received quite an education at the Alice D. Mac Phearson School for Girls.

The Steinle Men
Back row Gregg, Alan; Front row Bob, Frank, Dale

Anne, David Kent,
and Jackie in
our argument knots

Bob and
Jeannie
Burns

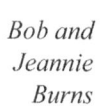

*Claude, Mark, Anne, and Dale
at Thanksgiving in our 30's*

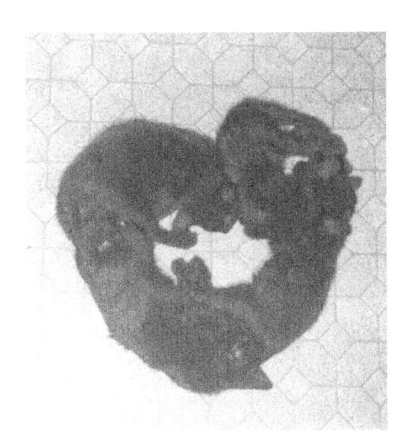

*Kitties in a Heart
Why not?*

Denise, Bob, Jackie Post

On Lee Dillon's porch. Top fave pic.

'Lambie' was thrown out the bedroom door every morning as an announcement of Ms. Thang's awakening.

Elizabeth thinking

Mid-life happiness

Happy until the end!

SECTION SIX

LIVING with the MENNONITES

It was the day of my release from the Alice D. MacPhearson School for Girls, exactly six months to the day of my entering. Ms. Kennedy was true to her word. A tall, almost glamorous woman had been assigned to introduce me to my next 'home' somewhere in Sarasota. I knew nothing of that area but I did know that this would be my first time out in the 'real' world without my Mother. (I can't count the time with Dolores and Frank, my mind was too fogged over.) That feeling of alienation was starting and had the woman not been extremely kind I may have floated right out the car window.

There's nothing on the memory board of that three hour trip except the stop for lunch at a nice Italian restaurant where I experienced some let's say, mental pauses.

(Hindsight thoughts…) Among the many wild things the mind does when trauma hits, apparently there can be a kind of arrested development. There were several things that I would hold on to from when Mother was alive and would not change until someone pointed out an alternative. Either I wasn't fully processing on my own or perhaps I didn't want to let go and lose yet another part of her. A perfect example of this was the tying of tennis shoes. Mother always bought me the style of Keds that when laced the eyeholes were pulled close together. The next pair of sneakers I tried on 'After' was made differently but I still thought they were supposed to pull together. That hurt my feet so I put them back on the shelf thinking sneakers were not for me anymore. I was in my thirties (yes, my thirties) when a boyfriend bought my first new pair, realized the situation and showed me how they were supposed to be worn.

Back in this nice Italian restaurant, the menu was in English but I could make no sense of it. And there was the pay phone. Having excused myself from the table to call Bob I found it had become a mystery as to how to use the thing. The woman, who was not just my driver but my intermittent Aftercare counselor, was patient and knowledgeable in guiding me through the blips and without any judgment whatsoever. SHE had the right job, unlike the fool during my jail time. The floating was well under control and I savored my first Eggplant Parmesan, still a big favorite.

I had a similar mental meltdown maybe ten years ago, induced by a week long 'vacation' of severe emotional stress. I was already at 'the edge' and only an hour and a half from home when my flight was canceled until the next morning. I lost it. I hate flying in general and traveling alone is scary for me. (My thoughts tend toward rape having been so twice more after the one described in this chapter). I fumbled around the airport for a while trying to make sense of anything at all and then as if from Heaven, I saw my friend Scott in the waiting area! I pulled my shell together and went over to

him. He was experienced with delays many times over from his traveling job and was not about to stay another night away from his family. I trailed behind like a battered puppy and listened as he TOLD the counter person what to do. A flight home that night was ours! Waiting in the bar, he watched sports while I downed three glasses of wine, returning me to a somewhat functional human being. He's held a high court position in my eyes ever since.

Scott

PINECRAFT

Sarasota was a pretty city then and it being on the gulf, the white sand found its way beyond the beaches to dress up the cracks in the sidewalks and around sign posts. Palm trees lazily waved as we drove down the aptly named Buena Vista Boulevard, lined with generously spaced well-kept middle class houses. Bougainville vines, giant hibiscus flowers and Elephant Ears filled in the gaps with vivid color and grace.

As we crossed over a small wooden bridge into the Mennonite village of Pinecraft, our time machine began its decent into the strange little town where I was to stay. Absorbing the sudden and weird changes in scenery, my worries of fitting back into the world I grew up in were of little consequence.

The first thing I saw was a little girl with long blond braids pinned to her head and wearing a long sleeved black dress, skirt to the ground with white collar and cuffs. She was playing with a group of girls all wearing the exact same thing. It was April in Florida.

We stopped to get a gift pie from a plain wooden building. The place was hopping busy inside and looking in the case at pie perfection, I could see why. Why so many men resembled Abraham Lincoln I could not see why. I would later find out that when a Mennonite man marries, he shaves his moustache leaving only his beard as the public indication of his new status.

Over that little bridge Buena Vista Ave. had become dirt and the few cars in sight were black with the chrome painted to match. I'm not sure if it was meant as derogatory or more descriptive but the term 'Black Bumper Mennonites' was used when referring to the sect that made up Pinecraft. A long list of controlling rules in religious sects, clubs, etc., can bring out the creativity of those who live on the fringes. Chrome on vehicles was not allowed. Paint over it and it's not chrome.

The hot weather lightened some of the stricter clothing rules. No zippers or belts allowed either so it was button fly jeans with suspenders. Trends often get started by the rebels of the world. I'm told todays' fashion of wearing your pants under your butt started in prison. Perhaps a silent 'Kiss my…" kind of thing?

We turned left onto a smaller dirt road lined on both sides with stark wooden buildings, long and narrow, similar to Jerry Brook's place. Along the river bank that dead ended the road were three standard cement block ranch houses. We parked at the middle one. Three smiling women in their mid twenties came out to greet us with hugs. They were Mennonites but opted for the cooler clothing, shorts, t-shirts and such.

Jeannie, Carolyn and Smack (from Smucker, not heroin use) were my appointed guardians and I was the first placement in the group home they were getting off the ground. We got on very well right from the start and as out of place as I now normally felt, I thought this might be okay.

As we walked through the carport to the side door, I noticed a flood line on the back wall about two feet up. Had the creek behind them once risen to that height? To wander off track again, I have yet to be involved in a flood and still find it an amazing yet horrifying concept. The resilience of the Katrina victims is truly something to be honored, especially those locked in the gym. I have shed tears more than once thinking of the woman who was raped in there. Having to endure such a violation while be dragged through a parallel nightmare takes a mighty strength indeed.

The house was tiny but I did have my own bedroom. My young caretakers all slept together in a huge bed in the other one. They were in the process of buying a bigger place and we would be able to move in when they returned from a prescheduled six week seminar on the care of 'wayward' teenagers. The new house was a mile back up Buena Vista... over the little wooden bridge and in the 'real' world.

But for now this was my 'home'. I was 15, family gruesomely shattered, five weeks jail time under my belt, the graduate of a reform school, an unprepared senior in a new high school and living with Mennonites. Floating was normal.

MANFRED MAN O' MAN

I walked the pleasant mile to school but took the bus out to Siesta Key to perform my maid duties at a Ramada Inn, the after school job I was required to get. That particular one didn't last long as even to this day cleaning and making beds is very far down on the list of things I want to spend any amount of time doing.

A funny night in that stint though; 'Manfred Man and his Wonder Dogs' were resting up during a tour and had joined the weekend Luau by the pool the hotel provided for the guests. I was serving drinks (at 15) and little plates of nibbles when I caught the attention of one of the band members. My shift ended when the Luau did but he and I lounged around the pool chatting for a few hours afterward. I had to be home by midnight so he offered a ride.

In the driveway he said goodbye with the longest kiss I've still yet to experience. There were no roaming hands, just one continuous kiss for what I'm remembering to be about thirty minutes. Soon after curfew the girls began to blink the porch lights off and on, off and on, off and on, until it reached a frantic (and somewhat hilarious) pace, none of them knowing how to deal with such a blatant breaking of rules. It wasn't a rebellious act, I just didn't know yet how to stop this guy. Finally it was over, we said a normal good night and he drove off. I apologized to the girls and confessed my predicament but they had little advice to give on the subject of bizarre romantic behavior at this stage of their lives.

AWKWARD!

On another notable occasion I came home from the beach one night fully blown out on one of the few hits of acid I would take in my life. We were all in sleeping bags on the living room floor as most of the furniture had already been moved to the new house. I crawled into mine but the acid prevailed. I couldn't stop reciting in full dramatic Arlo form a line from Alice's Restaurant…"Mother rapers, Father stabbers, Father rapers right there on the bench next to me!" I was also sticking my fingers through the imaginary tile ceiling grid I'd pulled closer with that relaxed eye trick. I would guess the girls began heavily counting on that seminar to give them guidance after that.

AND THEN THE ANGELS CAME…

During their absence, I stayed with the loveliest family I have ever met. The Weilers consisted of a husband, wife and two adopted children, Joyce and her biological brother. Joyce was exactly two years older than me and 183 years younger than Beethoven. She was beautiful with a constant radiant glow, big blue eyes, a natural curl in her long blond hair and a smile that put you instantly at ease. If she had any flaws the golden rays of love outlining her body cast a blinding shadow. It was she who showed me that my solid footing was nearer than I thought. It would still be a while.

Her brother was also gorgeous in the more earthly way looking like a white Native American. Blonde hair half way down his muscular back, his inner power showing its troubled kindness. He was four years older than her and so not around much. He drove a red and white electric car in 1971. I won't go into a tirade about big oil and their patent buying but it will be a blessed day when they are finally stopped of their evil behavior or at least when they realize as much money or more can be made by investing in less destructive energy sources.

The parents were a little older than most others like Mother was and the wife also had long blond curls but clearly dyed and perhaps home curled as well, possibly an attempt at publicly uniting her with her adopted kids. And what a loving open man the father was! Not a drop of anything to fear or disrespect. One night before dinner while saying the blessing he mentioned something directly to his God and also jokingly complimented his sense of humor. He was an easy man to be around.

Joyce confessed that she used to do a lot of drugs and lived the life that went along with that. I believed her but because of her radiant aura, I could not imagine it. She looked like an angel to me. She was an angel to me. She was my angel. I slept in a foldout bed in her room and we had great talks before going to sleep. She never mentioned her God to me but a 'presence' was there within her stories and in the way she handled herself. She had lived like the girls in reform school, but their tales were simply recounts of events, no ending or change. This was different and

My Angel

I was awestruck by her. Joyce told me that I sucked my thumb every night while sleeping. She had led me back to innocence.

TWO YEARS of THIS, THAT and the OTHER

Janie, Carolyn and Smack had secured the house and resulting from their six week seminar they were now fully equipped to deal with young 'wayward' girls.

Hahahahahahahahahahahahahahahahahahahahahahaha!

The new place had three bedrooms, two designated for two waywards each and our guardians would still share their giant bed in the third. They had their own bathroom and we had ours, plus a half bath and a fourth bedroom at the other end of the house which became the ironing room. Lots of ironing with a houseful of girls. It also had a family room, big living room, full dining room, and the all-important huge kitchen. Oh, and a laundry room. No room for ironing with all those baskets. LOTS of laundry!

Here's another example of a patent buy up. In this laundry room was one machine. You put your clothes in dirty and they came out clean AND DRY because of the added feature of a hot air blower. But that would eliminate the need for an entirely separate appliance to be sold. I imagine when the boys at Maytag and Kenmore figured this out they acted quickly.

The group home eventually consisted of the three Mennonite girls, each good-looking in their own style along with a tall blue eyed blonde named Lynn, an adorable 13 year old black girl called Mildred, a rough and tumble angry redhead with matching neck named Diane and me. Considering that variety, boys crawled out of the woodwork to check the action at this real life Petticoat Junction.

A neighboring family named Stone had three boys; two teenaged twins, Tom and Jerry (who I now recognize as highly favoring a long haired Jerry Seinfeld) and their younger brother Joe. Joe became a close pal, Jerry had matured and had a steady girlfriend, leaving Tom to excel at the role of Mr. Mischief. He confessed to peaking in our bedroom windows at night, proving it by telling Lynn of a freckle on her right breast. But he was harmless and funny like the other guys that came sniffing around.

Lynn's boyfriend was fine on the surface but he carried the jealous card. She was friendly with a natural smile for all kinds of people. During his insecure times he would fly into 'the rage' at her 'flirtations' and smack her around. She'd come home with a black eye or upper arm bruises from the shaking. It was easy to lie about it to our innocent guardians but the rest of us knew exactly what had happened. She always went back to him though. I thought she was crazy until my mid-thirties found me in a similar position, finally learning how one gets there and how hard it is to get free. It is however surprisingly easy to leave once you retrieve the power that was so meticulously and methodically taken from you. But that's another story.

JONESBORO-ROUND 2

Before Mildred and Diane arrived in the home, our 'authoriti' had planned a trip to Atlanta to visit a friend and announced to Lynn and I that we were going with them along with our pal Joe. We all rode up in Smack's never failing green Nova, kids in the back driving the girls to their edge with our continual singing of 'Too Late to Turn Back Now' by Tyrone Davis. Lynn, Joe and I were given a place on the floor in the little room with the dog bed and kitty litter, the tile softened by whatever our hostess could dig up.

The next night they were going out to dinner with their friend and allowed us to go out on our own into downtown Atlanta. As I said, they were naive. Off we went, two 15 year old girls dressed in the early 1970's hooker style get up of 'Hot Pants' and platform shoes. Sweet innocent trusting Joe in his tan slacks and light blue short sleeved shirt was our unlikely pimp. We went right down into the thick of it on Peachtree Str. in search of a little pot.

Standing on the sidewalk with 'RUBE' brightly written on our backs, a guy approached and offered Joe a way to get what we were looking for. Joe was to wait outside an apt. while he went in and scored. The guy took his money and never returned, of course. Left on the sidewalk, we began whining in our loud 15 year old voices about how long it was taking Joe to get back with our pot. Two boys were sitting in a big car in an earshot parking lot and offered to get us high. Problem solved! We climbed in and smoked a mind numbing joint. Lynn was upfront laughing and flirting with the driver while the 'gentleman' in the back hadn't even looked at me, let alone utter a word. I sensed trouble when we drove out of the lot, but I was so stoned I could barely function.

The car was a big luxury model with couches for seats and we were cruising down I75 for what seemed like forever. Maybe we were just taking a refreshing ride? Mr. Chatty still had not acknowledged my presence and Lynn was clearly enjoying herself. I put my face out the open window like a dog in the wind.

We turned right on to a road…WHAT? The sign said Jonesboro where my Aunt and Uncle lived…and then we turned again into a little patch of woods. Headlights went out, windows were closed, music turned up and Lynn and the driver got down to business. I continued to look out the window until I heard "We gonna let them have all the fun?" I replied, "Well, if it's up to me…." He said flatly, "You want me to get violent?" 'Nope' and I lay down on the seat. No kissing, not even one look directly at me, he just went about it.

There was a popular joke book at the time called "The Ceiling Needs Painting, Sam" with each page illustrating the bottoms of two sets of feet in the standard missionary position, a caption similar to the title underneath. I focused on what I could remember of that book until he was done and back to ignoring me altogether. For the next few terrifying moments I thought we girls might be killed and dumped in the woods to be found days later, my Aunt and Uncle doubly traumatized that it had happened in their backyard.

Miraculously, we were not only driven back to Atlanta but to our front door. (Joe was home safe, tired of waiting and unable to find us.) I understood right then. The driver had a good time with a stranger, a normal occurrence in those days and he'd assumed the back seat people had the same experience.

That's how it sometimes happens. I do not think it was my fault that I was forced into sex that night, but I take my share of responsibility by getting into a car with strangers, even though smoking pot with new people was considered a bonding thing back then. Had that guy been shown a fully informed view of women instead of as just a means for his sexual needs, he may have acted differently. In a vaguely similar situation with a true interest, my companion never even considered verbal persuasion, let alone physical. We simply got out of the car and took a walk on the beach.

Speaking of rape, I don't remember much about Diane the angry redhead, except that she had recently been brutally raped while hitchhiking. She had a racist background but made a few comments to the contrary. Maybe being raped by a white guy of her own ilk muddled her prejudice?

Lynn told her boyfriend what had happened except she claimed rape as well. He proceeded to beat the baloney out of her. I had no plans of telling my boyfriend Johnny or anyone else for that matter knowing I would be blamed (as the woman usually is…still today 48 years later) but he found out through Lynn's boyfriend. He barely blinked an eye.

Our physical relationship consisted of kissing and sometimes a little hand roving, but nothing involving the serious parts. During a more passionate afternoon, he suddenly declared "I'm not going down THERE!" Being a virgin it made me laugh. He also laughed and the physical part of our relationship sort of faded away. His rape reaction ended all parts of our connection and a few months later I learned that pretty Johnny was even prettier in his new gay life. Still, he could have cared a little.

MILDRED, MOTOWN AND MADNESS

Mildred came to live with us soon after the Unpleasantness in Jonesboro. By the time she was thirteen, she'd had two babies, both taken away from her. In her 'mood' which was understandably often, she would lie face down on the living room rug with the stereo speakers right by ears, sob quietly and listen to "Oh, Girl" by the Ohio Players over and over and over again. None of us knew what to do so we left her alone to cry it out one more time. One or more of us was always close by afterward.

Motown provided the reigning music of the time and also united us in the most joyous of ways. After dinner the record player would get stacked and the living room would be filled with Mennonites, wayward girls and sometimes a few lucky neighbor boys all doing the 'Stiff Leg' to 'I'll Take you There' by the Staple Singers or we'd act out 'The Way You Do the Things You Do' by the Temptations. Mildred had a big beautiful smile on her face on those nights. We all did.

It was during one of these after dinner mini raves that one of Florida's eight legged giants made a wrong turn from the hall and abruptly appeared on the crown molding above the dance floor. The high pitched screaming must have unnerved him and he jumped into the crowd, landed on Lynn's shoulder and quickly jumped back to the wall. We all went immediately insane.

Smack grabbed a baseball bat and went charging down the hall after it. Hearing the wild thuds against the walls and realizing we were out of harms' way the rest of us burst into one of those beloved giggle fests, the victorious Smack joining in a few minutes later. There were many other seemingly small incidences that occurred among this little group making laughter and love the ruling emotions. Well, not so much toward a poor spider, I suppose.

The girls took a stab at group meetings but were lacking in the knowledge and experience needed to let us go as deep as we did in reform school. They did get handed some doozies as wards for their first time out I'll admit but they had little dating experience and had each grown up within a loving family and community that still existed. We girls were all far away from any of that now.

Janie's family had money and grew up privileged so she sometimes couldn't feel the full weight of another's problem. Smack was reserved and guarded with her feelings and therefore mistakenly came off as a bit cold. She had a deeper insight than the other two however, calmer and more sensible by nature, so she took the mediator role most often.

Carolyn was fastidious with everything having to be just so. In one of the group meetings in which she held the leader stick, her beef was about the fact that someone had placed a wet washcloth atop a dry towel in our bathroom... OUR bathroom. She had a long way to go in figuring out what mattered to us at the time. She also had the energy of five people and needed the equal amount of nourishment to keep up with it. She ate six full meals a day without making a waver in her skinny little body.

Despite their bland seasonings from life so far, their importance to us was huge by providing love and a bit of stability while our own personal oceans were roaring on.

KNOCK, KNOCK

Bob and I kept in touch by phone but it was a while after my settling into the group home that we saw one another in person. He had taken refuge in New Port Richey and was sharing an airstream trailer with about 14 other people who randomly came and went. His job was good but demanding. Driving a cement truck six days a week kept spare time at a minimum which may have been a purposeful factor.

I was reading by the front window one afternoon when I heard a car pull up. Looking out, I watched a gorgeous guy get out of an orange Datsun fastback. A long sleeved maroon t-shirt was tight over his muscled torso, the sleeves pushed up to just under the elbow accenting those sexy working man forearms. His dark hair was an inch or two longer than a Dad's approval and he had the sex appeal of an Elvis or a Beatle on 'The Ed Sullivan Show'. Who was THIS and who was he here for? Four of us eagerly answered the doorbell.

Ruh-Roh, it was my own brother I'd been drooling over! He'd

lost weight, his glasses and he actually looked happy. I gladly let the other girls continue oohing and ahhing as we hugged and laughed out our excitement. We made plans for regular weekend trips to New Port Richey. Those visits meant the world to us, discovering that the bond of our friendship was now made of tougher stuff. Without speaking of it, we both felt the importance of us staying together for our own sanity.

THE MOD SQUAD AND MR. MILLER

My two main pals from school were Pancho and Stanley. Pancho had a light blue VW beetle and Oh My God we had fun in that thing! Together with these guys I blessedly experienced the much sought after 'normal teenage fun'. We'd pile into the bug and drive around looking to discover whatever the city had to offer. I've done some major league laughing in my time but this little trio could have won some awards. And Pancho knew where the real Cuban food was hiding in Sarasota.

Kelly was another pal. He was a singer and gaga over a Cher look alike in her midtwenties. We would see each other from opposite ends of the main hall at school and burst into some dramatic Humperdink song, meet in the middle and fake some movie love scene. He'd dip me, sometimes I'd dip him. These guys were very important to me.

This was 1972 now and things had really loosened up in some ways. Pretty Johnny happened to be black, but no one was concerned and I enjoyed not getting spit on. I did get sent home from school one day for wearing a halter top. The action and condemning teacher endured verbal protesting by onlookers. That was different. The offending garment was made from an unrevealing black fabric that bared only my shoulders. Scandalous! But off I went in the middle of the school day to change clothes.

The familiar handyman's truck was in the driveway when I arrived home. My entrance to the house was apparently noiseless and from down the hall I noticed Mr. Miller in my bedroom. He was the man we called to take care of anything one of the seven of us couldn't fix ourselves. He was Mennonite and unfortunately had a wife that brings to mind the term 'battle axe'. She was unnecessarily bossy and seemed to enjoy emasculating him. Somehow he remained one of the nicer people in the world.

Anyway, he was looking through my underwear drawer. Not smelling them, putting them on his head and dancing naked or anything remotely like that. He was just looking at them as he held them in his hand. He would have jumped off a bridge if he knew I saw him (and I mean that), so I backed outside and this time came in with gusto. I figured his awful wife had never let him see her when they were 'procreating', let alone partake in any sex for enjoyment or intimacy. Poor guy probably just wanted to see what a modern pair of underwear looked like. By the time I started down the hall, clanking about in the kitchen for a few minutes first, he was in the laundry room pretending to work on our fabulous washer/dryer. I stopped and chatted with him as usual, changed my horrifying blouse and went back to school. I hoped that his guilt wouldn't eat him alive. Guilt is such a hungry monster.

TINY TIGERS

I don't remember much about the classes I took except one called Mass Media. The teacher had a similar look to my current aftercare counselor. Shag cut blondish hair on a small framed tiger. Watch out anyone. Both of these women could and would love to kick your sorry behinds with their brains. They were proud, educated women with the inner strength that 1972 encouraged. Bother anything or anyone they cared for and you were history.

Fortunately, they both cared for me. My teacher cared for all of her students but she spoke to you as an individual and made you feel it. She was not one to follow the regular rules and curriculum of the school and as a result we went to Disney World for our final exam. It was its first full year open so the lines were State Fair length and then only for the very popular rides. The exam consisted of ten or so questions on the exhibits and rides we were required to take in. If we answered with more than the classic "I found it very interesting", we got an 'A'. I believe we all passed. And we had a ball. We had plenty of time to see and do more than our assignments so I was Disney World sated for life on that single day.

Dori Rickert was my aftercare counselor's name and I believe she cared quite a bit about me, although I could tell she also enjoyed the challenge of the fight. She was the perfect pitbull for the evil circus that was my case. She purposely kept many things 'in the files' and out of my knowledge with my protection in mind, but what I did learn was enough.

It seemed the police chief in Dade City was a 'man' named Nixon who was making it his business, along with the aforementioned nasty racist judge, to blame me for my Mother's murder. I discovered her body and my 'N.....-loving hippie s..t' was irritating their paste white skin, so let's get rid of me. Never mind that I adored my Mother, was a 14 year old peace preacher and had spent that entire evening elsewhere with many people.

I have never used the word 'Pig' to describe a police officer. It would be an officer I would first call in any dangerous or scary situation and am grateful we have such people that are willing to put themselves in harm's way for the safety of others. However, this Nixon 'man' actually did look porcine. He was large and round in the middle with pinkish skin and his blond hair was cut to a bristle. His nose was pushed up and each nostril was comically circular. (Haha, I made that last bit up for visual amusement, but his nose WAS pushed up). His fat face made his eyes squint. And to further set the scene, he was an amateur wrestler and carried that persona with him outside the ring. He was also soon to be arrested for dealing in child pornography.

This was who my 5 ft. aftercare tiger/pitbull had to deal with on my behalf. I'm not sure how long her battle with him went on but my appointments with her lasted until my stint was up at the group home. The visits were friendly and rarely disturbing, attesting to the fact that she concealed many gory details. Perhaps she was the one who discovered the pornography link. She kept me from having to speak to the porcine 'man', go into a court room or even talk to an opposing lawyer. They wanted me to see a psychiatrist, no doubt to have me committed, but that never happened either. You all know how the jaw of a pit bull shuts tight when it's got something. Well, that was my Dori Rickert. God Bless her where ever she may be.

NO SOUP for ME!

Our guardians were very caring people, but as I said also a little slack in seeing what might be important to us individually at that time. I'm not sure what the protocol for a high school graduation celebration is in the Mennonite world, but in the world I once thought I would be living in, there's usually a party afterward and in Sarasota it was to be on the beach with a big bonfire. I was looking forward to adding that bit of normalcy to my interrupted life but the girls had other plans.

Janie and a nice man named Bob had begun dating and had found love. It was obvious that the comfort level of their virginities had reached its max. They'd come in after a date to say goodnight to us, their faces beet red, Janie giggling at nothing in a screech pitch and Bob's fly about to blow apart. The time had come to end the agony, a June wedding was planned in Janie's home town of Goshen, Indiana and we girls were 'invited'. We did want to come but the idea was to whisk me away the second I walked across the stage with my diploma so as to make good driving time. I was terribly upset but it never occurred to them how important that party was so off we went. There was no final bonding with classmates, exchanging addresses or sharing information of future plans. No closure of any kind. I was angry and sad, but again to Noah Vale.

Goshen was similar to Pinecraft but followed the rules more strictly. The majority of transportation was by horse and buggy carrying multiple women in matching black dresses and gauzy bonnets covering tidy hair. Roads were paved but hours would go by between cars and most were merely passing through. The homes looked small compared to the huge gardens in the back. Janie's parents' money came from owning the iron horse business in town and their house was a demonstrative two story brick Georgian style with black shutters and lampposts lining the asphalt drive. It stood in leadership position at the T crossing of two main roads.

One afternoon in her Dad's speed boat we passed a horse and buggy filled with young bonneted girls clip-clopping along the parallel road. I remember feeling a little embarrassed by our noisy engine slicing through such a tranquil canvas. The wide eyed girls in the buggy seemed to be wishing they were in the boat.

MR. BOJANGLES

I graduated at 16 but had to stay in the group home until my seventeenth birthday so I got a job at a busy Mr. Donut to fill out the time. Since my hours were 7:00-3:00, I walked into the sunrise every morning. It got to the point that I barely noticed the houses and other manmade things along the way; the palms, live oaks and the myriad of blossoming bushes overtaking my view. The huge sun would rise up shining its glorious pink tinged gold over it all. Now that's the way to start the day!

I've kept a vivid memory of a jet flying across that morning sun. It looked completely out of place in the world I was walking through, much like I felt in the speed boat, except now I was on the other side of the picture, the correct side for me. I live in the country and still look at the natural world as the most important part of our essential being and happiness. Don't misunderstand, I treasure water from an indoor tap and adore the things electricity brings, but what this Earth offers up on its own I respect beyond measure.

My work mate was a career waitress in her fifties who did not like ONE BIT the fact that the new girl was young and attractive, a damn good worker and friendly to her as well as the customers. The capper was the length (lack of, rather) of my uniform. She should have talked to me about it because I had no idea I was giving a show when I reached up for the chocolate glazed. Do you remember the accepted skirt lengths of the early 70's? Only inches below big business.

My boss finally clued me in eliminating that part of her problem, but her dislike was well established. That was a shame because she had regular customers who loved her but her bitter attitude toward me showed through in her work.

One busy morning for some reason we were clicking quite well, doling out several cups at once and sliding plated donuts perfectly timed to stop in front of its intended. We crossed paths behind the counter, our shoulders and hips tucked to escape accident. We were performing the waitress dance perfectly and both of us were feeling the high of it. That is until my slide of a coffee cup went the inch too far and landed directly on to the lap of one of our regulars, the now quite startled handsome intern from the hospital next door. He jumped up and seeing the stain on his crotch spreading, I grabbed a dishrag and instinctively began wiping him down. The place erupted into laughter from everyone including the intern, except for my co-worker who could not stand all the attention I was getting. She tore off her apron and quit right there on the spot.

The baker always had a smile for me though. A happy man by nature but his smile was accentuated by nips of whiskey. He whistled a lively tune throughout his shift and would do a little one-two step when I came in the back for another tray of Bavarian Creme. He did his job well and I was unaware of his alcohol intake until I discovered the little bottles in the trash one day and asked the boss about it. He and the baker were pals even though they were decades apart in age. The boss (who enjoyed a similar breakfast) was in the position to give his friend a job and basically a life. It appeared a pleasant one at that, with his dog and a little place to sleep where no one bothered him.

SAFE HAVEN

My shift ended in midafternoon so I could run errands or grab some beach time before dinner. Or I could head over to the Youth for Christ recreation center Janie, Carolyn, Smack and a man named Doug all managed for the benefit of the local teens. This was a fantastic place and every town no matter the size should offer something like this for its up and coming leaders. The only thing religiously oriented about it aside from the name was the reading material available in an old brochure stand along the front wall. No one ever mentioned Jesus et al. unless a kid brought it up. That eliminated any pressure, awkward retreat from the subject or parental disagreements.

The building was a long rectangle of dark rough wood mimicking a Carolina hill cabin with a big wide porch running along the front. From the porch you entered a large event room with a movie screen and to the left was a smaller room with two pool tables and an office in the back. It sat on one half of a city block so there was a big yard with swings and picnic tables but it was the porch and the pool room that got the most use. Maybe it was the comforting closeness we all craved in the smaller areas.

The YFC's main function was to offer kids a safe place to go and if needed, a nonjudgmental adult to confide in. And that it did very well. Doug and some angry or frustrated boy were often found deep in quiet conversation at a far corner table or some teary eyed girl would emerge from the office with the beginnings of a smile on her face. I can well imagine the dire straits some of those kids might have gotten themselves into if that place wasn't there.

Doug was probably in his thirties and fit as a fiddle as his only vehicle was a bicycle. He would disappear for weeks at a time on some biking trek but at the YFC he was solidly present, filling the void of the missing father figure or other trustworthy adult male lacking in our lives. I often saw my Uncle Frank in his kind face.

The girls also did their best at being there for a kid, providing support without the tangle of an umbilical cord relationship. Even though her personal experiences in hardship were minimal, Janie once did a fine job evoking the much needed understanding between a pregnant teen and her indignant, stubborn parents.

The angry redhead had been gone for months, Mildred even longer. Lynn was turning 17 in a few days and had already found a little apartment for herself. I knew my day was coming up but was happy to have a few months left. The thought of living on my own was exciting but it also meant that ALL responsibility would become mine and mine alone. That realization put a small damper on the unfettered giddiness a 'normal' seventeen year old girl might feel about such upcoming freedom, the soft cushioning of parental support at her back.

THE STATE OF FLORIDA HEREBY...

...officially pronounced me an adult and solely accountable for my welfare the day I turned 17. Ohhkaaaay.

My Sugar Daddy (Mr. Donut) provided enough savings for my first apartment. I found a little house close to the marina and got a job at a restaurant by the bridge to Lido Beach making considerably more money as tips were now involved. I didn't have a car but what did I need one for? I could walk to work, the beach, the movies, the downtown five points and even though it was a few miles, I walked to the pool hall in the South end of town. This place was in the same style as the one I learned to play in 'Before'. Families playing foosball right next to a group of rowdy high schoolers. In other words, safe. My new home was a clean little dump completely furnished down to the dishes. After discovering the square plates in the kitchen I stated out loud, "Okay, if I have to take care of myself I'm going to eat a square meal every day". This was influenced by my Uncle Frank's cornball humor and also acknowledged the fact that if I didn't take care of myself there was no one else that would.

The food pyramid was much different back then but my education of real vegetables and general cooking began here. Dolores had firmly established her own influences on intake limits. I bought 'The Joy" and started baking my own bread. The restaurant I worked in had a killer blueberry pie and that became a special weekly treat. My neighbor was a midtwenties Harley owner who offered a second pair of hands if needed and was sincere about it. Lynn's own dump was nearby and I was making friends with a sweet boy from the pool hall. So far, so good.

OH, THOSE SQUINTY EYES

On a beautiful Sunday afternoon my helpful neighbor asked if I wanted to go for a ride with him on his bike. Nothing romantic or sexual, just cruisin'. "Sure, sounds fantastic!" We rode slowly along the beach taking in the scenery and discovered that I was a biker's worst nightmare. Leaning to the left when he leaned right, tense the entire time, that sort of thing. He was ever so patient and tried to teach me but my mind would not let my body respond properly.

And my balance is a bit wonky. Somewhere in childhood we went to the skating rink for the first time. I confidently strapped on my skates and immediately became liquid. I could NOT stand up on those things or even roll. Making it to the rink by handrail, I threw myself out there only to repeatedly fall and get up until the loud speaker blared out. "Would the chubby girl in the black t-shirt please get off the rink? You're in everyone's way." I crawled off, worm that I was. This could explain my horse issue as well. I've never had a problem climbing stationary things like ladders or trees and there's rhythm when dancing. Now after my leg accident it's even worse. I can get off kilter simply standing still!

My neighbor never asked me to ride with him again but he was still happy to help and Thank God for that. I opened my front door one night and there on the far curtain at eye level was one of Florida's giant cockroaches or possibly the larger water bug. I stopped dead and stared at him as he turned toward me. My memory has me seeing a neck, squinty eyes and a cigarette in his mouth but I know that can't be true. He lit out and flew steadily and precisely right into my face. Needless to say, I lost all control of my limbs and screamed at the top of my lungs. My neighbor came running out and a battle ensued for several minutes, his super hero cape unsmudged in the end. My fears were low level with him living next door.

FUTURE SHOCK

I could have used him as a neighbor in a later house I lived in. It was the standard two bedroom ranch with a bath in between and a tiny adjoining hallway. I was alone and coming out of my room when I noticed a massive spider covering the entire hallway's ceiling (not at all). I was supposed to walk directly under this beast so she could drop on my head, crawl over my face and birth her babies in my mouth? I think not!

The sensible side of me knew that this was never going to happen and that the poor thing had a worse fear of the gigantic pink creature below her. However the sensible side of me was, let's say inactive at the moment. I stood in the doorway desperately trying to jolt it into motion but to Noah Vale. My pal Sherry finally came home and upon opening the front door I raced out, bounced off the doorjamb and crashed into the sofa. "Spider?" she calmly asked.

God help us all if the bug world decided to use the power they hold over us. Does anyone remember seeing the '70's movie called 'Frogs'? It was a low budget put together that depicted that very sentiment. Campy and hilarious yet the message came through loud and clear what could happen if the nonhuman world united.

There is already quite a bit of organization and communication going on in that world. I'll tell you about one example but when you take the time you'll easily see something of this magnitude among the nonhumans around you.

Right around this time maybe?

I hope you remember this, Stephan. You were 4 or 5 and we were in your backyard swing looking out at the manmade pond that wound through your neighborhood. A gator popped up right in the middle of it with a dead duck on its back. It wriggled itself around until the duck was sitting upright. That accomplished, the gator sunk down hiding to leave only the duck at water level. Right then on the opposite shore another gator slid quietly into the water and positioned himself about 15 feet to the back side of his pal, also sinking below the surface. Both lay in wait for whoever might come along to investigate this duck. With that kind of teamwork it would be wise for all of us to gain a healthy awareness and due respect for all life forms on this planet. Or else!

BAD DOG

My job was in a middle level diner with an open kitchen and some fairly decent food. The weekend cook was always hung over to the point of pain. I can still see him placing that last breakfast plate for me under the warmer. The grimace on his face was as if his arm had caught fire from the grill heat but I now know it was from his pounding head. He was not anyone you wanted to be around, barking and biting as he did, and one day he tried to draw blood.

It was Sunday brunch and I had several tables that filled quickly after the church down the street let out. I could never balance that serving tray the way the other girls could but I was fast on my feet, organized and being the comedian, tried to get my people laughing and relaxed during their wait time.

The preacher must have had a particularly rousing service that day because the chatter was high and orders were big. Most of my tables were covered and content but on the way to pick up an order someone asked for ketchup. The beastcook saw me turn away from the waiting plate and lost it. Loud enough for the entire restaurant to hear, he roared out degrading remarks and a string of obscenities in my direction. Curse words have never bothered me even when said right to my face but I do not take disrespect lightly. After delivering that last order and apologizing to each of my tables, I took off my apron and walked out. As I opened the door the diners applauded my actions and the cook returned to his own misery.

I went to the beach for the rest of the day and even though my general situation was going well I decided that it would be a bump up if I moved over to New Port Richey with Bob.

HAPPY HOLIDAY

Bob turned 21 two weeks after my freedom (December birthdays) and received his share of our inheritance. The entire package consisted of the aqua blue Ford Galaxy and $5400.00 from the sale of our 'Murder House'. Bob got the car and $2400.00. He'd rented a comfortable little place in the back row of a redundant suburb called Holiday. He was secure with the cement truck job and had plenty of friends that I liked as well. It was an easy move on my part.

Theresa was Bob's close friend and also drove in his same company. She was a pretty, busty thing with a big heart and a big smile for everyone. She would often show that smile and her bust by driving topless. The cabs on these particular trucks sat high up above the other vehicles, so this was done mainly for home team morale. It was a happy place while she worked there.

She was visiting one day while I was trying to cut out a dress pattern and I absentmindedly complained about not having proper scissors. She excused herself and soon returned with a brand new pair of seamstress shears she had ripped off from a downtown fabric store. Big heart yes, and I sincerely hope her brain caught up with it.

Another female friend had a small child and Bob's closet was knee deep in toys for the kid whenever they came around. I discovered this one day after sliding open one of the doors and stuffed animals and trucks rolled out like a Macy's parade.

My first car was a little green Austin American and I spent most of my time driving back and forth to San Antonio/Dade City visiting friends. I would learn about general auto maintenance with this car by blowing the engine from lack of oil. If I stayed put, playing pool or beach time usually took care of the day. Not eager for employment yet, I basically ratted around until Bob came home from work.

Bob's habit was to end his work day with an ice cream cone from the neighborhood parlor. As the counter girl handed him the last scoop of a five gallon container of pumpkin ice cream, she flirted that he was the only person who ate any of it. I don't know why, but I've always found that endearing and wanted to share.

Danny was another good friend and a solid sweetheart. I began dating his best pal before I met him, so my crush on him was in silence. Both his parents were midgets (the accepted term then) and they lived in a trailer that they would open to the public for a fee. Angels were looking after that Danny Boy.

The neighbors discovered another friend well past midnight wearing a Superman suit and vacuuming the sidewalk in front of our house. Him I never met, but he certainly warrants a mention.

>>>>>>>>>>>>>>>>>>>>>>>>>>>>>>>>>>>>>

This would turn out to be the happiest time Bob and I would have together 'After'. I was learning my way around the kitchen so we ate actual food, money came from his job and my social security check, friends were in every corner and we were back under the same roof, our dog Judy included.

We were even lucky enough to have a tiny patch of woods behind the house that was home to a friendly raccoon family. On a regular basis, the Mother and three kids would scratch at the back door screen and join us for light refreshments and conversation, making for some interesting Happy Hours. Dad, a huge roly-poly with an obvious attitude toward humans, finally showed up and ordered his family back home. We missed them terribly for a while.

My brother and I were often found in the Hour of Happy, using one or more of the readily available material ingredients to drive us there as the emotional ones were not yet at hand. We had a little fantasy that we loved to embellish for laughs, usually after those laughs were already racing down the road. It started with us laying out the table for a dinner party. One place setting was oversized using a platter, meat fork, carving knife and so on. We offered only vague hints as our arriving company raised their eyebrows. The special guest turned out to be the domesticated Gorilla who lived in our garage. Hhhmmm, maybe you had to be there. Oh well, we had a great time thinking up endless tiny details and various scenarios that might happen and always, when we finally did introduce him, he took great pride in modeling his new yellow shorts.

Bob and I spent many an evening sitting at the kitchen table talking about everything under the sun, serious topics as well as the aforementioned silliness. Well, there was that one subject we didn't go near yet, both having thrown a cloak over it. But aside from that, we were in a Vulcan mind meld. It was the best of times during the worst of times.

AND WE'RE OFF

Early one morning I felt a tap on my shoulder. My sleepy eyes found Bob kneeling by the bed, his anxious face close to mine. "Talk me out of joining the Army." I should have tried harder. Much harder. Army life is not for everyone. The emotional devastation caused by our Mother's murder may have eventually mended, but during this time I witnessed a change happening inside my brother and not for the better. For some kids a warless tour of duty might be the ticket. The discipline, camaraderie, the responsibility and stability are all solid growing tools that may have been lacking earlier in life. But for others, an indescribable quality emerges... a 'distance' of sorts, like something has been removed. I don't know.

Anyway, off he went to boot camp and off I went to '809'.

THE '809' DAYS

809 was my address while living a completely untamed and deeply meaningful chapter of my life. I knew the house well as it was a regular stomping ground when I visited Dade City and Claude, Mark P. and Dale lived there. I remember the exact scene when I asked if I could move in.

The 'yard' was dirt with a big tree on the left side of the 'driveway', the car parked too close to the open door. The house had three bedrooms, one bath, a kitchen, living room and even a dining room. In its day it may have been a cute little starter home but at this point it had been condemned for years. The outside stucco was probably holding the place together. That and all the webs from the giant brown house spiders that decorated the corners. The place was filthy, broken furniture, boxes for tables, bare bulbs. The rent reflected the condition. I walked up and stood in the open doorway.

Claude and Mark were on the couch, an orange plaid Herculon throw away, and Dale was in the chair. The TV was on. They had recently gotten a 'meal' from the Royal Castle and Mark's Royal Burger was worse than usual. In disgust, he threw it at the window beside the TV. It stuck. The cheese like product they used was closer to glue than food and the rest of it wasn't even attractive to bugs. It had been hardening there for a few days and I thought it was hilarious and quite the statement. It was then that I asked to move in. It's an interesting study to note how priority levels alter when need/want does. All I could see was a place to live with three people I adored, Claude and I having been more than friends by this time. I saw it as a family of sorts looking after each other and I felt that's what we did.

809 and Mark Patterson

We were all lost for our own reasons and jobs weren't exactly abundant. The guys did pick up work here and there and I had my monthly Social Security check. It was $269.00 if I recall and I could make it last til the next one if nothing came up. As soon as it was cashed, I'd go to Ralph's butcher shop and buy four big thick steaks for us. They were only about $1.39 a pound so it really didn't dig into the bank. The grill was a rusty red wagon with an old fan grate on top, Mark's ingenious doing. A pile of dead wood was gathered for the fire. We'd sit on tree stumps, eating, drinking and laughing, a lot of laughing. We were royalty at the feast.

Somehow we all managed to find enough money to get to the bars in San Ann. It was party time, the time to be outrageous and wild and emotionally driven. It was also when I imposed my first rule of discipline…no drinking before noon…eventually.

San Ann's population was 483 and it had three bars; one liquor bar which was named after its owner Ralph, and two beer and wine places. One catered mainly to the Northern kids that went to St. Leo College up the street, so you could count on knowing almost everyone in the other two.

Our beer and wine bar was called John and Mary's and in the old grocery store my favorite preteen band was named after. It once supplied the little town with its necessities and was doing the same thing again but for different needs. The spacious building held several regulation pool tables along with foosball tables and a small stage with a dance area across from the bar. I heard The Outlaws play there once before they got famous but mostly the bands were derived from local talent. It could get pretty wild, but never dangerous. I can still envision Steve Wirt dancing and singing to James Brown's 'The Goodfoot' up on the bar and having a ball. Years later I was told he committed suicide, poor sweet man. I didn't know him all that well but he had a kind heart and I liked what I knew. I hope his sister Susie is a happier person.

DUDE WITH A 'TUDE

I would drink til the end, not yet thinking about limits and without anyone to suggest them. One of those huge brown house spiders lived in the front left corner of the bathroom for a while and I had to view it as a friend as I was in there often making room for more liquid refreshment. I succeeded and at least once shared my tears with him.

My routine was to buy a drink and put a quarter on the pool table right off the bat. I held my own by then and won enough that my few quarters usually lasted until I was too drunk to play a decent game. One night Richie was my opponent. He wasn't a true local but living there now. Richie was a tall handsome man, big shoulders under his plaid flannel shirt and really long hair that only made him manlier. He bought our drinks and we started our first game, laughing and openly flirting with each other with obvious intentions of making it a full night. I won the first game. No one else was up so Richie dropped in another quarter, bought the round and I won again. He was noticeably quieter and more serious during the third game and much less flirtatious, but I was still on the same track. I won again. Fourth game, no drink for me and he was just plain mad. Mad to the point of affecting his game and I won again. He threw down his stick and stormed out of the bar in a huff.

I was shocked! In all my pool playing days no one I'd beaten, boy or girl, had ever acted that way. I wasn't one of those 'in your face' winners either, that belittling behavior that guarantees a fight or at least words. It was just a game, for the Love of God. Anyway, my plans cut short and my feelings hurt, I went to the bathroom and cried it out to my spider friend. I was actually a little disappointed when he finally disappeared. Just a little, though.

JUST AN AVERAGE DAY

Ralph's was a different kind of bar. John and Mary's attracted the kids, but Ralph's was the place where the seasoned whiskey drinkers gathered. A tiny cement block square with one small pool table and jammin' every night. Old weathered farmers, young cowhands, hippies, women of a certain age, all kinds would be slapping each other on the back and playing pool. I don't ever remember a fight, although they would have been taken outside so I may have missed a few. Helene's presence never raised an eyebrow either. It was thick in the 'Give Peace a Chance' period and quite a magical time in San Antonio, Florida. I still feel blessed to have experienced that little town through those years. The hippie ideals were guiding me through times when my Mother should have been raising me and many of those beliefs are still deep within me today.

When we weren't in San Ann or in some orange grove howling at the Moon, we'd do our partying at home. One night we were all drinking red wine and doing some sort of athletic competition. Claude was a muscular guy and showing us by doing a round of pull-ups. All of a sudden he spewed a fountain of neon pink on the back wall. We all had a great laugh, it got cleaned up somehow and we went back to our evening.

A classic moment was immortalized by Dale. He was returning home in Claude's car, the massive steel '55 Chevy. It was blue and white and each seat could hold about seventeen people comfortably. The problem was that it had no brakes. You'd have to put a can of fluid in before heading out and hope to reach your destination before it all leaked out.

Claude and Mark were outside by the front door when Dale came rolling into the yard too fast. He screamed out a forewarning and grabbed a branch of the tree, trying to stop two and a half tons of metal like a Flintstone would do. Of course that didn't work and it crashed into the front of the house, knocking the kitchen counter away from the wall. It didn't go completely through the wall so that's how things stayed. A big rectangular dent in the outside wall and the counter jammed up against the refrigerator. Thankfully, Dale's arm didn't get ripped off during this adventure, but I don't think that occurred to us at the time. It was just another hysterical episode added to the family cartoons.

I use the term 'kitchen' loosely as not much happened in there in the way of cookery. The refrigerator was usually empty and the cabinets played house to bugs trailing strings of dust. There was no cookware except one little frying pan and a small pot. Occasionally someone would make a bacon sandwich or a burger. A rabbit was shot and grilled but it was flecked with metal and inedible. I lived on Campbell's soup that I bought daily for about .29 cents from the convenience store a few blocks away. I still eat a lot of soup but now it's homemade. Soup is good food and that is a good slogan.

Another 'renovation' we managed to do was in the bathroom. The wall next to the sink was shared by Dale's bedroom, which was 6' x 6' and painted flat black. Oddly, the outside wall was a gigantic picture window. It could have been anointed 'The Terrarium' I suppose, but we called it 'The Elevator Room' and proudly wrote its name and a few other descriptive words on the door, as one does. On the bathroom side, the sink faucet leaked and sprayed a continual mist over the shared wall. A simple washer might have righted it but I'm not sure any of us had knowledge of such things back then. One day (or night, it often blended together), Mark got tired of being sprayed in the face while brushing his teeth. He expressed his feelings by leaping at the wall. It was much softer than anyone had realized and he fell right through, unleashing the 647 mice that had set up housekeeping. It was a laugh riot and fairly disgusting. I believe Dale began packing for his Mother's empty house right then.

MY ROOMIES

Mark was an absolute wild man, but he was also an extremely caring person. I figured he had convinced himself that his life was not going to be a long one because of his heart condition. That would enforce both traits. We were getting back in the car after rounding up what food we could afford that day when he presented me with a little red rubber bird and said "Here, I was thinking of you". It is still one of my most prized possessions. One drunken night, we found ourselves starting to go beyond our platonic friendship, but out of his loyalty to Claude, Mark showed the strength that sobered us up before it was too late. That was a lesson I had not yet learned and am forever grateful to him for it.

Who remembers the movie 'Zachariah'? The James Gang did some music for it and Mark was a roadie for them at the time. We were so proud of him when they asked if he would be an extra on the set. No details, just giving him his propers.

Claude, as previously mentioned, was equally as wild, also deeply caring and had become more attuned to the Natural World than most. There is a great comfort and peace to be found in that world. Moving away, I asked for his address. Under his name in my little book, he wrote "Contact with the Gentle Motion of the Forest". That is another prized possession.

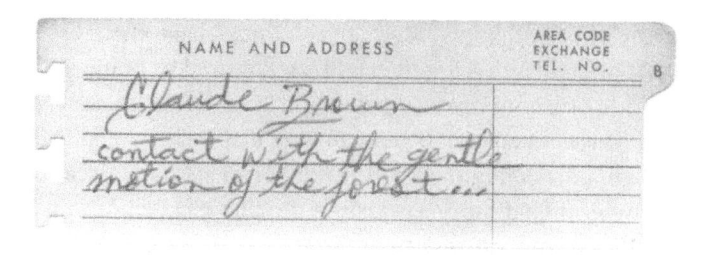

I wouldn't say Dale was a wild man but he most certainly had a huge heart. He became a very active and honest Christian early on in life and coupled with his job of driving vehicles from one state to another, he managed to do his part in spreading the Word of Love across the country. He often picked up hitchhikers and left them changed or at least doing some hard thinking, whether on a religious note or not. See, Dale had a habit of relating ALL the thoughts on his mind about a single conversation topic. You knew what he was thinking, why he was thinking it, when he developed that particular thought, if it made him hungry, if you needed food, what he knew about the workings of the stomach and so on. He would often drum his fingers together while doing so, perhaps creating a rhythm for the endless words to follow as they tumbled out of his mouth. He provided a free and open study of the mind.

Dale could also put an entire loaf of French toast into his very normal sized body. I would occasionally make breakfast for us over at his Mom's place before starting the job he hired me to do. We would find great entertainment in watching his belly expand to regulation hoop size.

A small golden brown dog arrived, a stray like the rest of us. Claude took him under wing. Someone saw the letters O.R.M.Y. as highlighted on Dale's bedroom door sign and it became the dogs' name. Ormy, the dog.

THE OIL CRISIS

Dale's adultless house naturally became yet another hang out for us all. A few of my friends' parents at that time were nowhere to be found and Dale's mother was on that list. She was alive and well, just not living in her home for a reason I never knew.

This was no ranchburger. All the public rooms were large with high ceilings and arch ways, each bedroom built with privacy in mind, two complete baths and a front porch. One could see care and attention in the details of construction. When I mentioned to Dale that I could cut a decent line with a paint brush he hired me to paint the whole interior of the place. What a fabulous job! Completion time was 'within reason', my piddling money needs were met for a while and it fired up my creativity. Unfortunately, I doused one of the bathrooms with a little too much decorative fuel for Dale's taste.

He had gone to visit his Mom for a few weeks and I thought I'd surprise him before his return. The colors in a Standard Oil station bathroom had called out to me. The previously painted tile rose about four feet high all around, a perfect canvas for the deep rich Cobalt blue I had fallen in love with, the higher walls in a matching pale blue. The main bathroom completed, I was thrilled with the vibrant (oil-based) outcome. Dale was Certainly Not! It didn't take long before I saw it through his eyes as the gas station bathroom it mirrored. I was so focused on color alone that I initially failed to see the full result. The ever patient Dale never got angry though and even allowed me to continue with the rest of the house. Dale would be choosing the paint.

Before Facebook made it so easy, Dale would be the one to reach out to those of us who had strayed from the pack. He showed up at my shop one day, twenty years later and twenty years back now, when a car delivery brought him nearby. His sky blue eyes were illuminated by a very large halo of long white bushy hair and beard complimenting his never ending grin. What a happy day that was for both of us. We talked with no deference to the gap in time. I've been away far longer than around this group of people but the importance and love I have for them has never wavered.

MASTER CAPES

I had strong yet confusing feelings towards James. First, as I said before, he was someone to solidly admire. Everyone did. He was talented, witty and understanding of what was happening worldwide as well as with his individual friends. And then there were those moments we shared the night of the murder. I can still feel falling into his eyes, words unnecessary as we grasped the severity of what had happened. That's a specialized closeness not to be tampered with. And then of course, he was a boy and I was a girl and I just plain liked him. Confusing.

We were sitting on the back steps of Dale's house one day singing 'Seems like a Long, Long time" (Well James was, I was

imitating a bullfrog) when Claude drove up, having been assaulted by an insurance salesman. He had signed up for 8-9 policies for tiny amounts of monthly money, but forever. He was happy about it but James and I were hoping it wouldn't make him feel immortal. Claude was already physically fearless in general. He and Mark made quite a pair.

Claude defying a garbage truck

SILLY GIRL PROBLEMS

I met Sherry during this time. Helene had asked me to come with her to pick up her friend after an appt. in town. She had borrowed a van and after parking, Helene got out and opened the back doors, motioning me to come back and get in with her. There were some blankets and maybe a pillow or two and it was probably all carpeted because of the times. The feeling was very comfortable.

Helene and Mark. He's just playing.

Sherry's appt. was with Social Services, but Helene didn't say what it was about. As we sat leaning against the front seats small talking and waiting, the viewfinder of the open back doors framed a picture of the town we lived in. It didn't look friendly to me anymore. Someone here had murdered my Mother. Was it the man coming out of Rexall's? Maybe it was that woman carrying the Belk-Lindsey bags. I bought my sewing supplies in that store. Now my Mother's murderer might be shopping right next to me. My new idle thoughts.

Sherry on a much different day.

It wasn't long before Sherry showed up and in full sob. She climbed in and Helene's arms rocked her until the shaking stopped. Finally they sat back and Sherry whimpered out that they had taken away her children. She was 21. Mildred came to mind. We all cried, sharing our burdens. After a while sighs of the dissipating weight were heard among the sobs, even an occasional chuckle. The van must have been glowing from the emotional cauldron boiling within, relief radiating in the steam bubbles escaping from our combined stews.

We stayed in that van until there were more laughs than tears and spent the next several years helping each other keep it that way.

>>

I met Pete at one of 809's parties. They were never planned affairs with cocktails and appetizers, more like some kids came over with a bottle and a baggie and stayed for a while. Anyway, Pete came along with a mutual friend. She had rolled in to town from the Midwest in a gigantic white Cadillac. She looked and sounded very straight and timid, but she was one serious party girl, let me tell you. And brave. She had a 'charge ahead' attitude about life. My attitude was often led by a deadened battery. She introduced me to Key West on a "Hey, let's go to Key West today" whim. She

Pete

knew some people there, so seven hours later we started a week of nothing but fun. There are benefits to living like the wind.

She also drove me to a psychotic gynecologist's appointment in Tampa. The 'man' caused bruising on the skin of my abdomen from his internal exam! On the way home with me finally comfortable and sprawled out on the back seat, she stopped and picked up a group of hitchhikers overloaded with huge backpacks and other on the road items. I was shoved up next to the door with a pot handle poking my side and the smell of the unbathed in my nose. There are also detriments to 'wind living'.

New people would randomly appear by way of friends or simply passing by and stopping in. One such person was a mad woman who called herself 'Kwichie', (from the root word 'quiche'). Talking nonstop and high on some hallucinogen, she tried to convince me that she had fled the Allman Brother's compound and the entire state of Georgia after discovering a pair of severed heads under some coats in one of the bedrooms. It was obvious she was embellishing for entertainment and it was pissing me off. Actual murder comes with plenty of real details. The true story was her walking in on two lovers while tripping what was left of her brains out and was ousted because she'd already overstayed her welcome. She was nearing that point with me at our first meeting. Drug crazed babblers were not our style.

ONCE WE KNOW

It seems more attention grabbing to relate the insane stories and depraved behavior. Look at news casts. Start with death and destruction, erotically detailed sex scandals, the political nonsense of the out of touch, then with a chuckle treat the selfless act of a homeless woman as a puff piece, not to be remembered or taken seriously.

My stories here may not be as entertaining, but my emptied soul was savoring the emotional bounty that was served up during these '809' days. Yes, we were wild and high, but our brains were in fifth gear and our feelings were raw. We were passionate and empathetic, raging, joyous and full of sorrow all at once. Everything was considered and we were sorting out what really mattered. We were searching for the shoreline after life had thrown us overboard.

Aside from our own personal stories, our whole generation seemed to be taking stock in what was being handed down to them. The basic foundations in a belief system were being questioned. Perhaps wars were not the proper responses to disagreements between countries but vile and conducted as money makers at the expense of poor people. Maybe a woman was more than Mrs. Somebody Else. Other cultures and races might be different, but should that automatically make them inferior or to be feared? What were the real truths about the forming of the United States of America and where should we place our pride once we knew?

We were blessedly placed in the middle of a mostly peaceful revolution that brought about a new vision of everyday life. Without money and starved of love, we were learning we could feel rich and sated on the true finer things this world offered and what we ourselves had to offer. We were beginning to discover our own worth and what was truly worthy.

SECTION TEN

GERMANY, 1973-'75

After boot camp, Bob was fortuitously picked to stay in Frankfurt and work at Gutloit Kaserne, the receiving center in Europe for all incoming troops. His M.O. could have taken him to some

Godforsaken hillside for winter recon training and the like, but with this assignment, we could live together again and in a normal German setting away from the base, so a 'plan' was decided upon.

Packing for this was fairly simple. After Mother was taken, the house and its entire contents were sold without any thought given to what we kids might deem as important. Everything that made up the home I grew up in was gone.

But as I was still on the planet's surface (was I?), I had once again gathered up some personal belongings; a Featherweight sewing machine, a few tools, clothing and some albums. My material life fit into a trunk and a suitcase. Back then you could call the airline and have your ticket reserved without paying until the day of your

Gutloit Kaserne, inside the courtyard. It was built with one entrance in and out.

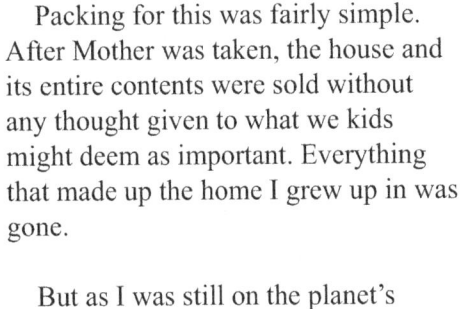

flight, so when we arrived at the counter, I handed over what I took to be the entire charge, only to find that each bag had a cost as well. The trunk alone was an extra $150.00, which paying for was out of the question as the suitcase had taken most of my cash. Claude offered to ship the trunk over and I boarded for my two year stay in Germany with one suitcase and $2.00.

The plane was a 747 and felt more like a hotel than a mode of transportation. I'm not a frequent flyer but the planes I've been on since could be compared closer to riding inside a toothpaste tube. This beast could seat an entire Mennonite family in one row. The lighting was dimmed to 'homey' and everything was plush and comfy. Only half full which would never happen today, that trip provided luxuriant stretching room for all aboard.

Soon we were sailing along, not a care in the world. First class was everywhere. Food, drink, pillows and blankets were being offered by the ever smiling stewardesses and a large screen lit up to show a star studded movie. Headphones were available for $2.50. Shoot...50 cents short.

As luck would have it, a young soldier wearing headphones and carrying an open bottle of Gordon's gin sat down next to me. He passed out shortly after so I helped myself to his headphones and even had a nip of his gin. I often depend on the kindness of strangers.

The flight was long and somewhere high above the ocean we hit turbulence so rough it knocked the stewardess to the floor and caused needle like nerve jabs throughout my body. Nonetheless, we arrived safely at Rhine Mein Air Force Base on the outskirts of Frankfurt around 8:00 a.m.

Dressed accordingly for the early '70's, my travel suit consisted of black hip hugger bellbottoms, a black halter top (only the bare shoulders, remember) and big platform shoes. My purse was one of those flat Moroccan styles of woven yarn with a rope strap. It was first to be searched at checkout. I.D. okay, money...$2.00? The checker shot me a quick glance. Next, through a small worn area at the top, she promptly pulled out a bag of pot. WHAT!? I never bought pot, barely smoked it...one of my roommates must have hidden it in a moment of paranoia. Panic welled up as she unzipped my suitcase. There were my albums all nicely protected by my under things. That was the entire contents. Sighing, she eyed my silky black eveningwear and dryly asked "What exactly do you plan to do while you're here?"

Not seeing the obvious humor at that moment, I burst into tears from thoughts of multiple years in prison spiked by those scary TV commercials about getting caught with dope in Turkey. Whisked away to airport security, I was seated in a corner for the next six hours. The eight people in the room never spoke to me or even hinted at what my fate might be. I periodically sobbed and nervously wrung my hands thinking they were all preparing my incarceration. The reality was that they were all busy with other things and were having me wait for the two Army related cops required for my situation. When they finally showed up, one looked like Elliot Gould which I found comforting. The larger comfort came when he told me that I owed $24.00 in fines and we could be on our way. WHAT!? That explained the curious looks I was getting all day. What a waste of good anxiety.

Okay, so I made my European entrance, TA-DA! Now off to find Bob. The 'plan' we had devised about joining him in Germany was just that; join him in Germany. There were no set dates as I had to live by the 'answer the door quickly when opportunity knocks' rule. The money was in my hand that day so off I went. He learned of my arrival when that now sober soldier went through his line at the base (kaserne) and noticing his name tag said "Hey, a girl was on my flight with the same last name." WHAT!?

Bob promptly got leave permission and headed to the airport where he was simply told that I had been arrested for drugs, the officer failing to mention how minor the infraction was or that I was sitting in the back room. He spent the rest of the day trying to track me down in every police outpost in the greater Frankfurt radius.

Meanwhile, after being discharged, Elliot and the other officer located my brother's address and drove me to my new home. It was their job, but they also wanted to collect the $24.00 from Bob that they had so generously paid in my behalf. We raced onto the Autobahn where there are, Aaaaauuuugggghhhh!!! NO speed limits. Suddenly, I was being tossed around like a Hackysack in the back seat of an up-ended tuna can on wheels with Elliot Gould driving 100 miles an hour.

Completely disheveled and disarmed, we finally pulled up to the address alive and well, ThanktheLordGodAlmightyKisstheBeautifulEarth. The 'front' door opened into a porch that hung slanted off the back of an apt. building. Double doors led into a living area where sitting in clear view on the table was a large ashtray holding a few half-filled hash pipes. Perfect. Elliot pocketed one and told me to forget about it (Were they even cops?) so I went to find my room and unload the suitcase.

Oh, this is just a closet. How about that door? Nope, another closet. The kitchen was so small I could touch the opposing walls with my outstretched arms in any direction without taking a step. The bathroom was tiled in around a chimney which took up all but a sliver of floor space between the tiny shower area and a child sized toilet/sink. There were no windows except on the front of the porch. Two years here? 809 may have been a dump, but there was room to breathe. Bob arrived shortly after us and Elliot and company left with friendly waves, their money and a new pipe.

Bob and I were best pals so the craziness of the day was not something to get up in arms over but to be heartily joked about which is exactly what we did. I eventually asked him to do some 'splainin' about this true to form hole-in-the-wall he thought would work as our home. The sleeper sofa was my bedroom, its cushions to be used for Bob's bed on the (yet to be discovered) unheated porch. The back of the sofa flipped over into a permanent 45 degree angle for a rock hard pillow. Opening the matching rock hard bed revealed an uneven hinge which formed a ridge that ran horizontally at my hip line. I was not happy.

Seeking comfort, I decided to take a shower and get into some real clothes. Yes, I did notice the small pink tank next to the small pink shower and assumed it was the small pink heating unit the water passed through, not what held the entire available amount. Hair and body in full lather, the water suddenly turned an ice cold that came directly from the tap root of Germany itself which was solidly imbedded in an underground glacier. My brain shrieked from its shriveled state and every nerve simultaneously experienced the sharpest ice cream ache in all of history, no exaggeration.

We stayed through the next several months to fulfill the lease requirements, spending evenings hosting a hash & beer laced 'Spades' party, the card game of choice for Bob's soldiers buddies. He and I were always partners and still having that Vulcan mind meld, we did our share of butt kicking. Two of Bob's work buddies lived above us and were equal matches so egos were kept in check. We managed to enjoy ourselves despite the twelve second showers and Flintstone like sleeping conditions.

Bob had purchased a Citroen, one of those crazy liquid tuna can cars. The design of this thing looked as though they had taken a Volkswagon and cut out the center section, leaving the sides cartoonishly flat. It would never have met the safety standards of the States, but over there the fact that it swayed freely as it roared down the highway was A-OK.

Germany has a fabulous public transportation system, the strassenbahn, or strass, as it was commonly referred to. The streetcar is mostly above ground and the tracks were often in the middle of a street. Shortly after my arrival, we were tuna casserolling home from a party and as we rounded a corner the car slid on a section of track and fell flat on its right side. We were in the same position, but sideways now. Bob looked calmly down at me. "Are you alright?" "Yes" so he opened his door and climbed out. I was about to do the same when gravity slammed the door shut. For a moment my imagination took me to dripping gas and an explosion. I scrambled wildly, scratching at the door. Bob was overcome with laughter, opened the door and I cannon-balled out.

Safe now, I let the humor overtake and this is how the Army police found us minutes later. They swept him away and left me standing in the middle of the road in the middle of the night with the overturned car. I had no idea where I was but started walking. Hours later I eventually found my way back to the base where Bob had been taken after his arrest procedure. We lost the car and his license for the duration, having to rely solely on the strass system. Never once did we feel limited.

LESS IS MORE

It's curious. The Army recognizes your Mother-in-law as a dependent, but not your own blood sister. That oddity turned out to be in our favor however, as I got paid in Marks through my work and 'had' to shop in the German stores rather than the PX where most of the other Americans felt 'safer'. A richer education for me and we never lost money through the exchange process.

One thing I garnered being among the locals was a firsthand perspective of a people with groups of foreign soldiers roaming their sidewalks day and night. It's frightening, to say the least, even in peacetime. The truth of it, in this case anyway, was that these young soldiers traveled in groups because they were afraid of being in a foreign country. It was Bob or pal Justin, both having put effort into learning German, who played spokesperson, the others too shy or insecure to speak. Still, the sight of troops brought fear or hateful looks, especially from the older men, toward the Americans.

The American Express Bank catered to hiring the Army wives so I headed over. I was told by one of those wives that a middle aged hound dog was doing the hiring, so I should wear my shortest skirt when applying as there was no place else to work. I believed her. He got an eyeful of thigh and I got a job. I even got the partial week stint that I always asked for when working for others. He stayed behind his desk and conducted himself properly, I sat there with my panty hosed legs crossed, answering his questions and looking straight into his wandering eyes. Quite the innocent whoring and I left doubting I needed to do it at all. My advisor friend obviously had some self-esteem issues.

A child could have done my job and may have in some countries. I sat in front of a small machine and typed in the routing number on the bottom of a cashed check. Checkaftercheckaftercheckaftercheckaftercheck. My boss was a German beauty in her prime and her wisdom of the business world, including all its unfairness of the time, was apparent. She was a pillar of strength yet gracious and open. The way she dealt with her boss, the hound dog, confirmed that the length of my skirt was an unnecessary perk for him. I came to feel completely at ease with her despite her role model stature and my reverence.

My first day at work was similar to my arrival in Germany. The morning was uneventful, but then the lunch bell rang. I went across the street to San Remo's, a place Bob and the boys often frequented as the American Express was around the corner from the base. Bob had recently shown me that 'less is more' in the dessert world by the purchase of a simple cookie in the bakery next door. My choice was some gloppy, drippy sugary mess. He offered a bite of his and the flavor explosion was amazing. Mine was nothing but sweet.

BOSS!

I ordered lunch and tested a German beer, thinking it 'light' as I was a liquor drinker. After downing a tankard of double strength lager my error weighed in. Wobbling back to work and a half an hour late, (oh, lunch is only a half hour?) I was obviously tipsy. Feeling the direct stare from Boss I sat down and got right to work. As it was the early '70's, I lit a cigarette and promptly caught my trash can on fire with the tossed match. I received another direct stare, but this time she covered her mouth, the smile still showing in her eyes. I put out the fire and quietly went back to typing for the rest of the day, my admiration of her born.

COME ON, ROCK HUDSON?

The office was eventually moved to a newly renovated space with a greatly improved desk design. Boss had her own office closed off by windows to the work area. We now had a floor manager, a young Army wife with long red hair, black rim glasses and a profound love for Elvis. So profound that she was the first person I thought of when he died. I'm sure it took an unprecedented toll on her health and possibly her marriage for a while, but during my time with her fireworks shot from her soul whenever his name was mentioned. We did it often and with accompanying pictures simply for the fun of her reactions. With the help of a gossip mag groupie in our midst there was no short supply of Elvis trivia. That wife and her similarly afflicted husband provided all the latest celebrity updates to spice up our lunch break but I rarely believed any of them.

DANGER, WILL ROBINSON

Someone introduced me to an over the counter liquid speed, an appetite control 'medication'. It sharpened my senses and made my mindless job interesting. Every check, every number was important and the challenge to increase my productivity never dwindled. I loved it, it wore off by my shifts end at 2:00 and Thank God I eventually had to leave the country.

MY KIND of REALITY

Across the Main River from the base was an unspoiled part of Frankfort and I'm forever grateful I happened upon it. Too few of the other Americans I knew ventured out of the designated Army safety arena. A section of the road along the river bank was cordoned off every Saturday for street venders. It was built from gorgeous old cobblestones and huge arching shade trees dipped their leaf tips in the water from the edge. Prewar architecture lined the other side. The only thing remotely close, and I mean remotely, to that outdoor market I'd seen yet was at the county fair with its open sided trailers filled with glitter and orange plastic being pushed at you by scary men yawning from boredom. The venders here were selling actual artwork…their own artwork. Paintings, handmade pottery, leather bags, clothing you could never find in a store. Violins sang out under skilled musicians' hands and not one accosting sales pitch could be heard. Now THIS was right.

One perfect sunny morning while absorbing the quality of it all, I noticed a girl about my age leaning against the railing under a tree. We looked like soul sisters with our long hair and hippie attire. I was excited at the prospect of making a German friend and smiled at her with hope. She returned it with a harsh glare and looked away. I was taken aback by her unwarranted meanness and kept walking, disappointed and hurt.

What was her reason for such hostility? Was she the jealous type? Perhaps she saw me as yet another intrusive American. Had she returned the smile she would have found her boyfriend was of no interest and our ideals probably similar. Instead, she chose to put hatred and distance into the world and between us.

INFERNOS

The closeness Bob and I shared made it easy to see that there was an emotional disquiet within him. I was worried but hadn't a clue what to do about it. His anger was reaching a new level of intensity. We had both developed quick hot tempers, mainly over illogical situations or acts of stupidity, especially when we brought them on ourselves. We'd roar with our trumpet voices, bang our fists on the nearest inanimate object and if together, quickly cave into laughter at our own folly.

Once in New Port Richey we were headed out to dinner and caught by a red light. I was driving the little Austin American and a cement truck was behind us. The light changed and the truck sprang forward, bumper crashing through our rear window. We simultaneously charged out of the car surrounded by fire and bolts of lightning staring the driver down into a cowering pool behind the wheel. In minutes though, we relaxed. No one was hurt, the car was still drivable and since it was the same company where Bob worked, things could be taken care of without all the red tape. The poor driver was a trainee and his foot had slipped off the clutch. An accident. We were all enjoying the comical size difference of vehicles when the police arrived.

That's usually how our anger behaved. But as time went on during his tour, I could feel an under bubbling in even minor

161

incidences. He also directed it at me a few times with the rage meant for a rusted bolt or a banged knee. Neither of us were dealing very well with our Mother's murder. I wasn't dealing with it at all, staying high most of the time to suppress the tornado of emotions. But there was no guilt in my storm like there was in Bob's. I reiterate; guilt is a hungry monster. I watched my brother being eaten alive by it over the years. Do what-ever it takes to rid yourself of it as quickly as possible. Determine the source of the guilt. If it's warranted, make amends no matter how complicated. If not, spit it out and luxuriate in the new lightness. It could save your life.

MARK

Billy came into the picture and we started dating, so to speak. He was from cowboy country and followed the classic male/female double standard. Because of my Mother's influence some of his actions seemed outright silly and most completely unacceptable. One argument led to my question "Do you mean that if I broke my leg you wouldn't make us dinner?" He replied in a matter of fact tone, "Well, I'd get a sandwich or something." I sensed being a tad too skinny in this relationship.

Despite the mismatch we stayed 'together' for several months. He was outwardly a nice guy, good looking, liked to laugh and I suppose the biggest factor was that he was part of the group.

He was there when I opened a letter from home. A few sentences in and I burst into an uncontrollable sob unable to speak for a while. When I finally explained that my friend and 809 roommate Mark Patterson had gotten killed in a car accident he was only annoyed. "This is why you're crying, over another guy?"

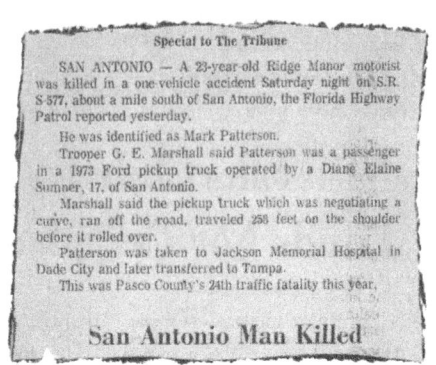

Special to The Tribune

SAN ANTONIO — A 23-year-old Ridge Manor motorist was killed in a one-vehicle accident Saturday night on S.R. S-577, about a mile south of San Antonio, the Florida Highway Patrol reported yesterday.

He was identified as Mark Patterson.

Trooper G. E. Marshall said Patterson was a passenger in a 1973 Ford pickup truck operated by a Diane Elaine Sumner, 17, of San Antonio.

Marshall said the pickup truck which was negotiating a curve, ran off the road, traveled 258 feet on the shoulder before it rolled over.

Patterson was taken to Jackson Memorial Hospital in Dade City and later transferred to Tampa.

This was Pasco County's 24th traffic fatality this year.

San Antonio Man Killed

I was on the other side of the world with the stupidity of a jealous boyfriend for 'comfort' and no closure so the grieving entered my vividly realistic dream world. I had just begun reading 'Gone with the Wind', usually right before drifting off. Night after night it was the same dream and as sick as it was, I began to look forward to it because Mark was alive again. Well, sort of. I read only a few pages at a time and successfully kept it going for months. Basically, it was my job to drag Mark to safety through the scenes of the book. This affected me so deeply that I can still pull up some of those images today. Closure is very important for forward movement in this life. I missed having someone there to help me achieve that.

JOHN EMERSON

Needless to say, Billy and I broke up. Not before I got pregnant, of course. Abortion had reached 'The Pill' status in America but still illegal at that time in Germany. However it's fully loaded socialized medical system offered a competent hand for having a healthy baby and finding it a loving home. Our culture had Billy assuming I would move back to the ranch with him and begin our lives together. I was not raised thinking in those terms and rudely, I'll admit, laughed at the prospect of me as the doting wife he was imagining. It didn't occur to him to take sole responsibility of his baby. In any case, I was not in any state of mind to raise a child, so I opted for what I thought was best for the baby.

While the adoption agency inexplicitly offered no emotional counseling, it otherwise seemed thorough and caring for all concerned. I was allowed to name several specifics about the manner of the receiving family. I asked for little lean toward any one bent hoping for the free thinking powers Mother had gifted me. No myopic religion, Atheism included. Quality of life, respect for the earth's gifts and concern for others should be driving forces, not the greed for money. Racism or supremist attitude of any kind was out of the question. A family was chosen. One parent was a pro bono lawyer and they had another adopted child as well as two of their own. The agent assured me that they fit the bill on my requests and I felt I could believe her. I entered the first and middle names the parents had chosen on the birth certificate, minimized the vices, ate what I thought to be healthy and exercised regularly. A 9 lb. 4 oz. healthy boy was born on August 7, 1975.

The birth had its moments. I was not asked about drugs and was given a spinal block. I was also given a prior pain med making me unaware of what was involved in such a procedure and almost rolled over on my back on the needle, the nurse flying from her seat just in time. This was apparently a teaching hospital, so when the crowning began a group of young male interns stepped out from behind Curtain Number One to watch. They applauded as the baby arrived, saying their congratulations and so on, me nodding and tipping an invisible hat. It was a happy moment, what with the beginning of life and all, until a nurse whispered in German and the smiles and good wishes stopped, eyes no longer meeting mine. My legs were still in the stirrups for the added emotional punch.

Then something else began to happen. "What the… another baby? Oh my God, what is THAT?" I was completely ignorant of the placenta; the pot roast that followed the birth. Now that was shocking!

My hospital stay was 5 or more days. I was given ice packs to reduce my milk flow while the other Mothers nursed their love bundles in our shared ward. It was an impossibly hard time and needed the parking lot to wail out my misery and throw up from the depression.

LOAM LOVE

Bob was a busy boy in his own fashion. John was a new work buddy and he and his wife Laura joined the Spades games, both at the tiny place and then at the new two bedroom, real kitchen, living room, full bath and dining room apartment we had moved into

A Strassenbahn

Pin the Drug on the Junkie

outside Frankfurt. Bob hung a large poster of a Gorilla in his room, keeping that happy time alive. It became a solid entertainment destination so there were always enough people to play cards or Pin the Drug on the Junkie, a timely adaptation we came up with. We hosted Thanksgiving dinner that year for as many as could fit in the place. Our tiny burg of Harheim was just outside of Bonames, five kilometers from Frankfurt.

Off topic for a moment, I was awed by the lack of urban sprawl. The city would end, farmland and unspoiled country side would take over, another tightly knit town, then more natural expanse. Gorgeous. A communal garden dotted with little sheds butted up to Harheim and was mainly used by the city dwellers. A few folks tended their spots during the week but on the weekends it became a grand social occasion. Folding chairs and food baskets with plenty for sharing would fill the porches. It was a place to relax, garden, laugh with their weekend neighbors and throw their cares by the wayside.

On the road back from 'planting' the pot seeds.
A rare sunny day. We were almost transparent.

Pulled by the magnetism of it, I would take walks close by and trade smiles. The soil itself was so rich and black you could smell it in the air. I had only lived in sandy Florida up until then making the contrast phenomenal.

We threw some seeds by a creek one day in a half-hearted attempt to grow some pot and promptly forgot about it. When we did finally return we found huge 6 foot bushes lining the bank. Pot was not commonly grown at the time, hash being the preference. We simply chopped them down, dragged them right through town and up to our apartment as if a normal garden crop. It wasn't killer weed but a different buzz from hash, so worth the 'effort'.

Bob and Lee

Bob and Laura

Hugh Hefner

Apparently, I decided to replace Jesus that night

BOB'NSTEIN

Bob and Laura started feeling something more than just friendship and quietly began feeling each other. Not quietly enough apparently because at a party at their apartment I was let in on the secret and unfortunately so was John. He responded by punching Bob square in the eye. Bob refused to wash up, leaving blood all over his face and his swollen eye unbandaged for all to see on the strauss ride home. When he caught a little boy staring at him, he growled "I'm a monster, leave me alone!"

Years later a girlfriend told me that Bob would occasionally refer to himself as a monster in rough situations. The load of misplaced guilt for Mother's death seemed to be causing this underlying belief that he was some kind of menace to society. Many men (some women, too) have a false pride that keeps them from asking for help. They stomp around displaying how strong they are physically to divert attention from whatever is keeping them emotionally weak. I call it 'Roostering'. We all probably have a little bit of it but don't you find it detrimental in a large capacity?

He and John still had to work together while the couple separated and Laura moved in with us. I doubt their marriage would have lasted for the long haul anyway as John and Bob remained friendly and he even came over to play cards, the exes seemingly unconcerned about their recent past.

Laura once told me that she could not stand to be alone for even five minutes. I've known other people with that same fear. One reason might be that they needed the distraction from their own thoughts, too disturbing to handle alone. I'm not sure what it was in Laura's case. She always had a smile on her face and never hinted at any underlying misery. She was smitten with Bob and would sit at the other end of the sofa watching him read. No book for herself, just happy to watch him. I confess I'm pleased in saying I've never been that smitten. Yikes!

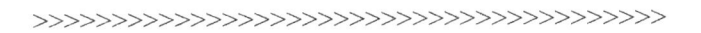

Bob's tour was coming to an end so I headed back to San Antonio as he had to move back on base for a final blast of Army Education. I shipped off my trunk, packed my suitcase less provocatively and while dressed more casually, I wore the still popular ankle cracking platform shoes. On the last step of the planes exit ladder, I tripped and fell flat on my face. My return to America.... TA-DA!

SECTION ELEVEN

BACK to SAN ANN

No home waiting, I went looking for a roof. A mistake named Jeb introduced me to future friend Jim. The three of us were in the same predicament so we rented a trailer. It lasted one month. I couldn't stand Jeb or living in a trailer from the first day and it showed. Jim was AWOL so the combined 'atmospheric pressure' did not induce relaxing at home. Funny stuff, Jeb told me I pounded my head into the pillow every night. S'pose I had some inner turmoil. He thought I was crazy and left me alone, Thank God.

There was some ratting around after that. A few nights were spent in an old Airstream Helene knew about. A place to sleep, no water or electricity. Some beer and chips had been left there and that was breakfast. I remember thinking that where ever I was headed, it was Not Here.

Aunt Leola's Kitchen came into play and often. It's been a dream of mine to open a little place like that, calling it by the same name to honor that sweet saving Grace. Another source of food sounds like it came straight from an Alan Jackson song. Every so often, Helene and I would take the long walk down River Road and with $2.00 buy a 'mess o' catfish' out of a little wooden shack owned and operated by the same man who caught the fish that morning. Years later, I was taken to a trendy new Southern style restaurant in NYC; pickled okra as the free appetizer, grits, hush puppies, collards, etc. as the sides and catfish was a very popular entrée. It was quite entertaining watching people gobble up what perhaps they themselves recently considered 'garbage food' and paying through the nose to do so.

A bedroom at Sherry's house opened up with my name on it, the house where my spider fear had me bouncing off door jambs. She had two sisters and a brother who stopped by regularly bringing friends and future husbands with them. That family has always had

Sherry and my new puppy 'Keith,' named for Mark Keith Patterson

a great love to share and it made for a happy and lively place.

A friend stayed with us for a while who made her money from sex. I had come in the front door as one of her clients came out to leave. It was Otto. We'd not seen each other since the murder. Our eyes locked, reliving the purchases of my Easter dresses, helping Jerry Brooks with his shoes, the grief and sadness, and now… what to say in this moment? I'm sure his heart was breaking thinking I was also a 'working girl', but I'm sure he was also dying of embarrassment inside. We should have cleared the air.

THREE 'TRIPS'

Our friendship didn't end but my living with Sherry did when an apartment next to Helene's house in San Ann became available. It was a duplex, the other half rented by handsome Terry, the bartender out on Lake Iola. He always avoided me thinking I would come on to him but he had no worries. I just liked looking at him. His car was a classic Batmobile, long and black with fins above the tail lights. I still carry a mild interest in owning some fabulous fun car like that. A convertible with fake fur seats for a road trip with sunglassed girls, scarves rippling in the wind like freedom banners.

A visiting hitchhiker stopped by to play for a while. He was a handsome thing with long hair (hippie law) and took up residence in a yurt out in the woods. Yurts were seen as exotic then and we were duly impressed. In reality it was made from giant pieces of plastic he'd shaped with fallen logs, but to young anarchists it was 'righteous'.

He showered at Helene's and managed to nail most of the girls around him. After discovering the 'collective' we named him 'The Cloud' as that was how his lovemaking felt. He was so gentle that one could barely feel his presence. The nickname was not born from malice or disdain so he was still welcome for dinner and other gatherings but none of us ever went back for 'seconds'. That applied to his cooking as well. He once proudly offered to fix up a big pot of stew starring the rattlesnake he'd caught. Um, you can cook it here Steve, but it's all yours. I am a carnivore still today, but given that as a choice I'll take another helping ofs me spinach please. Toot, toot!

SAIPAN MAN

Sherry and I were in Helene's yard soaking up the sunny afternoon when a side walker passed by with an open fifth of Smirnoff's in his hand. We let him know the consequences of being that public so he decided to stay and play in the rays with us.

He had come halfway around the world from the tiny U.S. Army occupied island of Saipan to attend St. Leo College. The interior walls of his family's tiny home were made of curtains, dividing the space for him, his parents and several siblings. Short statured with soft black curly hair, his skin was a beautiful light brown highlighting perfect white teeth. He kept those teeth in good shape by chewing fresh coconut every day and was worried about them as coconuts weren't as readily available over here. One of his thumbnails was about an inch long, manicured and sporting a neatly drilled hole. This was a sign of marriage. On the wedding night after the new couple fell asleep, a sibling would sneak through their curtain and drill through the nail as an announcement of the union. (Does the Mennonite groom shave his own mustache?) He came alone to do his studies, kind hearted with a good sense of humor and we welcomed him into our little group.

Sherry and I decided on a camping weekend in the Blue Ridge Mountains of North Carolina as we'd driven through coming home from the annual Fiddler's Convention and found them stunning. We thought our new friend might like to see more of the country and invited him along. We loaded up my aptly named Plymouth Satellite, the loose steering giving it a hovering quality, and off we went. Not long into the drive, he asked when we were going to get there as he had a class at 5:00 that day. Fortunately, he found as much humor in his confusion as we did so we continued on as planned. He was astounded by the changing landscapes and endless hours of the journey. You could almost see the concepts of distance and space expanding for him. He never got bored and exuded pure glee with every new discovery. We all returned richer for the experience, but as much of a nature girl as I am, tent camping leaves me cold. I confess to opting for above ground porcelain every time.

FRIDAY NIGHTS

Most of the time it was the three of us; Sherry, Helene and me. Both of their Mothers had died during this time period, way too young and for Hellish reasons. We were wild. Wild with heartbreak and the rage it brought on. Wild with freedom, wanted and unwanted. Wild with the desire for love.

Tequila was the drink and dancing was the energy expenditure. The three of us would kill a fifth and hitchhike the 30 miles to Tampa to either Skipper's or Loser's (A bar named 'Loser's? Really?) and go nuts. We'd dance with each other but occasionally some brave boy would sneak into the scene to be later tended to, usually by Sherry. She was the one who found sex to be the most equally relatable activity in our trio. Drinking usually negated any physical feelings I may have had. Unfortunately it also invited false emotional feelings to take over.

But we all loved to dance. By night's end we were spent, sober and ready to hitchhike back home for a sound sleep. Somewhere during this time, Helene got pregnant and gave birth to the future singer Faith Evans. This curtailed her partying but Sherry and I continued our nonsense with full force.

Helene and Faith at 1 year

ONE ANSWER

My Social Security check was going to end unless there was future schooling so I enrolled in Pasco-Hernando Community College. If history were to repeat itself, this might prove tedious. Fortunately, Sherry and Jim shared my Biology and Psychology classes, doing our homework together and finally providing me with a few helpful study habits. I remember to this day the feeling of reality coming through my floating and the closeness I experienced with them as we tossed questions and answers back and forth, our minds focused only on the subject at hand. It was a blessing to close the door on the darkness.

WHAT JUST HAPPENED?

Upon turning 21 I received my inheritance of $3000.00. Since Bob and I partied away his riches I thought it best to do something sensible with mine. We would buy a house!

Aided by Mother's 'Outside what box?' methodology, Bob and I went to San Ann's only realtor, Midili Insurance and Realty, and stated our intent. He showed us two houses. One was over a hundred thousand dollars and nothing to our liking, it being very traditional and 'shiny' with neighbors much too close. The other one was perfect, as if it had been planned for us. Maybe it was.

There was one piece of furniture in the house, a chair from our original home that our cat Sandy used to sleep on. It was a '50's swivel style in the salmon color that I had picked out when we had our furniture done. My jaw dropped. It was like Mother herself was sitting right there saying "Here you go, kids." I had to be sure it was our chair so I turned it upside down. Sure enough, the old teal sateen was sticking out beyond the staple line of new fabric. Speaking from my upholsterer's podium, I can say that the old fabric shouldn't have been left on, but in this case it shook my world. Or rather, helped to settle it.

The house was a mile outside of San Ann surrounded by orange groves on a full acre with a separate garage out back. A porch had been closed in providing a perfect addition for my sewing set-up in the front bedroom. All the rooms were spacious and there was even a washing machine. The colors and 'upgrades' were cheap and tacky but we only saw a home. The price was a mere $20,000!

The chair gave us no option but to tell Mr. Midili that we had to have the house. He supplied the name of a mortgage company in Tampa and we arrived on time for our first appointment. We faced a pretty blonde woman in a business suit with polished fingernails that matched her lip color. Her desk held organized files, staplers and stampers, a gold pen set, the framed picture of hubby and children. All the signs of a normal successful American life. She faced Wild Child siblings showing no signs whatsoever of normal successful American lives. We politely greeted one another and she asked what she could do for us. We told her of the house we wanted to buy and asked what we had to do in order to accomplish that goal. She said, and I can quote her, "First you have to get jobs." Her voice was as true and honest as if she had said "Down the hall to the left." Okay, Step One!

We shook hands and thanked her for the information letting her know we'd return. A fast two weeks later we were facing each other again. I had found work at St. Leo College's golf course and Bob was hired on in a friend's surveying company. We told the successful American woman that our combined income was $7.35 an hour and again in her matter of fact tone she accepted that amount as sufficient to buy the house. We signed the papers and became homeowners without even a down payment. My fortune was used to put in a new well. Since we had nothing to compare it to we had no reason to believe this was unusual. Could it have been this easy in the mid 1970's?

Sandy's favorite chair being present in this particular living room seven years after being dumped in a second hand shop became of high value in my expanding view of life. Of all the gin joints…

WORK IS FUN!

That golf course job was nothing but great but I certainly had to prove myself in the beginning. My immediate boss Bobby had no problem with a 'girl' but the owners, the golf pro and everyone else involved (or not) had severe doubts. My test was to break up the old concrete driveway leading from The 19th Hole to the barn. The plans were for asphalt and the 6" thick slabs needed to be removed. I was

On that snow day. See the asphalt? That's where the concrete was!

to break them up with a sledge hammer, load the chunks in a single tire wheel barrow, steer it down the hill behind the barn and dump it. It took three eight hour days with no breaks except for lunch. I caught Bobby's smile occasionally which provided extra steam for my little engine that could.

I must confess that after that first day of hard and dusty work the ONLY thing I wanted was a beer. Beer is not my drink. Don't like the taste and carbonation has never been my friend. But that first afternoon at 5:01, I headed straight to the store, pulled a tall boy out of the icy barrel readied for the town's working men and UNDERSTOOD! Nothing else could have been as satisfying as the rough bite of that beer washing away the concrete and muscle soreness. That one golden elixir had the elevating powers to allow in the feeling of life's pleasures.

After those first three days I was readily accepted by everyone (except the owner's wife). My boss had me doing everything; mowing greens and fringes, pruning trees, anything that needed tending. He put me in charge of the restaurant landscaping and used Latin terms when teaching plant names. He respected me and showed it. It was the same with his assistant. Both of them were young and happily married. We not only became a great work trio but friends. I felt safe.

The course was on a hill and driving around on a three wheeled Cushman cart was a blast. I still want one today. It's an open two seater (no doors or roof) with a little truck bed behind. When one got too old for our uses they would donate it to St Leo's across the street which is why a tourist driving through San Ann might see a nun or two racing about in one.

The mornings out on the course were Heavenly, my office glorious Nature. You golfers will get this story. I soon found my name on the schedule to change the greens holes. Relocating the hole in a fresh area on the green every few days keeps the grass uniform. Switch dirt plugs, drop in the metal cup and you're done. Coming up on the seventh green I saw that it had two levels. Never having played the game I decided it would add some interest if I cut the hole in the slanted part of the ground connecting the two levels. I went about my work proud of my newly imposed challenge but when I went up for water the dining room was filled with angry golfers. "Who the Hell put that hole there?" "Blew my whole score!" and so forth. The golf pro and now my pal quickly escorted me away from the ire and explained the problem with a secret laugh. I snuck off to change it knowing full well that he could have made that shot with his eyes closed.

Most of the course was on a Florida hillside. A creek bordered the bottom in front of some woods that also went up one side, Hwy 52 was on the other side and the buildings were at the top. One morning the golfers near the creek suddenly began racing up and screaming bloody Hell, especially the ones on foot. The gigantic gator that lived near the water had apparently decided to take a stroll. He was old, still managing nicely with only three legs, and was merely looking for a spot to sun himself, though I could see where a 13 foot alligator might be disturbing if too close. Bobby knew him and guided him back down the hill with the Cushman but it remained quiet on the first nine until new and unaware players showed up.

The Sunshine State had one of its rare freezes during the first winter of my work span. At days end we left hoses spraying fragile trees to coat them with a protective layer of ice. The next morning was a view of Nature I'd never seen before. Gorgeous clear blue icicles sparkled in the sun. The entire course was covered in a glistening white blanket. Dark leafless branches proudly hailed to the sky under their white outline. It was magnificent!

Bobby suggested we go sledding. Do what? We tethered a huge piece of cardboard to the back of a Cushman as our sled and off we went, flying down the hill and eventually off the cardboard. Ice went up our noses and down our pants, but nothing could numb the exhilaration of that day.

A few years later and new resident of my home now, I was invited on a sled ride down Libe Slope on the Cornell campus. Skip Davis and Larry Paciello had me sandwiched and again off we went. Hhhmmm, something was different. The highly polished sled rails seemed to take more naturally to the thick layer of snow than the rough surface of cardboard over slick grass. As we breezed passed a low flying plane I became…pensive. Another difference was that there was a road at the bottom of this hill with cars on it, parked and moving. On the golf course there was a shallow creek with only a tiny chance of an uninterested gator in our path. High speed crashing into metal is not on my 'fun things to do' list so I sat out the remaining rides getting my thrill from watching those two beautiful, crazy men have their own kind of fun.

Part of the sandwich, Larry Paciello

Bobby was offered a more challenging job with better pay, etc. and he took it along with his right hand man. They both deserved it but my pals were gone! Their replacements left me lacking so when the next opportunity came knocking, I opened the door.

MEETING the FUTURE

Bob had decided to become a civil engineer (Dad's influence?) and mystery to me, managed to get himself into Tampa's University of South Fla. Maybe his genius IQ got him another scholarship. Driving back from school one day he came upon two girls hitchhiking. They were out jogging and had had enough so he drove them back to their apartment, which happened to be a stone's throw down the road from our house. The previous year Marie and Jeannie Burns had come to visit their sister Sheila who was attending St. Leo. The hoppin' little town of San Ann called to them. They were stepping out into the world and the idea of getting away from the cold winters in Binghamton, NY was warm chocolate sauce on the freedom cake. Being neighbors in a town of 483 San Antonions made it easy to become fast friends. Marie and I were cut from the same tiny wash cloth and Jeannie, well who couldn't like Jeannie? They're good people, those Burns'. They soon joined up with Dennis DeVine and Helene, who were already making music together, and formed the girls' first band, 'The Spice of Life'.

They were following the best weather for a few years by returning to Binghamton to avoid the stifling Florida summers, but at one point they moved permanently to nearby Ithaca. Cornell and Ithaca College are both influential in the town but the local population consisted then and still now of a large number of talented musicians, artists/crafts people of all mediums and inventive entrepreneurs. People seem to take pride in whatever they do. The atmosphere is creatively charged in all manner of activity.

Marie suggested I come up for a summer visit and see it all for myself. The next opportunity! She also mentioned the high number of handsome men roaming about. Bob had zipped through college and had himself taken Marie's travel advice only to discover his talent at the sound board for 'Fantail', the killer Ithaca band the girls were now in. I took the month of August as my first visit.

To get there, I drove my newly purchased 1966 light blue Volvo, the rounded one that looks like a cartoon drawing, and noticed that Volvo's seemed to be THE car of choice. I fell in love with everything I encountered, the richness of the architecture, the lush landscape, the ease of the people and the independent thinking that seemed to prevail. Marie was right about the handsome boys. The ones that would eventually become our friends were crowned "The Handsome Carpenters" by many more women than they would ever know about!

BODY CHANGES

Late one morning and back in San Ann, I was in Ralph's parking lot picking up my car from the night before. I ran into a friend and was chatting it up when Jim drove up with the news. Bob had been in a horrible accident.

Calling the number Marie had given Jim, the nurse's blasé voice yawned out, "Yes, Mr. Steinle has been in an accident. I can't tell you much more." "Will he be alright?" "Well, he lost an ear." "Whhhhaaaattttt!" "I'm sorry, I can't tell you any more". Click.

Marie met me at the airport. In the hospital parking lot she handed me a shot of tequilla. "Drink this and no more." The elevator doors opened into the waiting room and out rolled Bob. His entire torso, neck and head were bandaged mummy style including his right arm which was held up by a board. I could only see half of his face.

Marie was right again. I needed that single shot. Waves crashed through my inner body, but the outside shell stood solid. He grunted a little laugh. Helpful, as I was losing it fast. We exchanged some words, but he was clearly not up to it and the nurse took him away.

A quick recap of what happened... Bob and pal David Kent were driving home on Saturday night. A drunken fool appeared in their lane coming at them head on. David was driving and quickly went left to avoid him. At the same time the other driver finally noticed he was in the wrong lane but Nothing Else and veered right. The two passenger sides of the cars collided. Bob was spun around in the seat and his left ear, not the one closest to the door, was sheared off his head by the passenger side window frame. The spin broke his arm and damaged his torso; broken ribs, tears and major bruising, but no fatal punctures. He was lying on the ground when a car stopped. As the Fates, the Universe, Mother, God, Buddha and/or Random Coincidence would have it, a nurse was driving. Her first thought was that Bob was dead.

Bob suffered pain from this accident for the rest of his life, partly because the surgeon foolishly removed two side by side ribs for ear replacement material rather than staggering them. This left the ribs on either side of the gap an opportunity to catch on each other and whatever else got in the way when he bent over. I'm not sure which was worse though, the physical or emotional pain. I sustained an injury with permanent damage and it was five years before I realized how much it had affected my psyche. I felt vulnerable and let it guide my actions. Once I became aware of this, my mental strength came back. I'm not sure if Bob ever got his fully back. His injuries were far worse. On top of everything else.

After that initial hospital visit, Marie dropped me off at Bob's girlfriend's. Jackie lived in a second floor apartment overlooking Ithaca's first health/vitamin store. It wasn't long after my arrival that I dropped to my knees from pain in my left side. As if led by the hand, I went to that store. The first thing he asked after hearing my symptoms was if I'd recently experienced any trauma. I told him about Bob and his thoughts were that I might need a big dose of the B vitamins, adding that stress knocks the B's right out of you, the other main culprits being smoking and drinking. He also explained that the weakest part of your body gets targeted during an upset of normal function. It all made perfect sense and replenishing my B's took the pain away, physically anyway. From then on, I began to incorporate natural solutions to the treatment of my physical ailments.

That weak part of my body was found by a reflexologist I had recently made some clothing for. Giving me a quick demonstration of what his profession was, he found something (in my third or fourth right toe, if I recall) and simply said "You need to go to the gynecologist". He had horrible bedside manner and was obnoxious in general but he was right about that. The doctor discovered fibroid tumors. I was still working at the golf course which offered full Blue Cross/Blue Shield health insurance so off to the hospital I went.

My left tube and ovary were removed and my stay was several days. The morning after surgery a knife like jab went through my gut. Asking the nurse what the heck was causing that she drawled "Probably gas build up from the pain killers". She informed me that taking them wasn't required and that the gas was probably causing more discomfort than any coming from having my abdomen sliced open. I love her still today. Soon I was completely pain free and pacing the aisles like a caged lion. My fellow inmates were amazed at my progress yet through their fear of questioning the process remained at the mercy of the 'pain relieving' Sodium Penathal and its intense stabbings.

LANDLORD LIFE

I was missing both Bob and Ithaca so we decided to rent the house out for a while. Our first tenant was the daughter of the realtor who sold our 'Murder' house. She stole everything I owned which was packed away in the locked garage. The second tenant was a friend whose boyfriend was a goat farmer. I'm not sure how they lived but it took some time to get the goat smell out of the house. Considering our luck as landlords, we both returned to San Ann to regroup.

THE THIRD TENANTS

A couple of pompous asses named Bee Bob and Prince showed up at Ralph's one night. They were highly educated (and happy to lord it over you) and decided the tiny town of San Ann was a good place to grow bales of pot and make their fortune. Bee Bob was an apiarist, more ape than anything. Prince had long red braids and fancied himself a Norse God. He was not.

Before my brother went back to Ithaca he rented our garage to these two posers with the plan of growing pot in it and splitting the money four ways. I was not involved in the making of this plan. Bee Bob and Prince were lying. Since I was the home owner and living there, I would be held fully responsible if caught. The fear in this knowledge increased a hundredfold when soon after the operation was in full swing the orange grove behind us was cleared for the site of the new elementary school. A trailer was moved onsite for vandalism prevention by a live in police officer. Our once hidden house was now wide open for viewing from the back side…where the garage was.

I rarely went into the garage disassociating myself as much as possible, but I had a message to deliver. Holy Moly! The plants were over my head and the buds were the size of Papayas. This was going to turn into a LOT of money. Especially since that $20.00 ounce was going for $200.00 due to the new strains and richer markets now on board.

I never trusted either of those guys. Bee Bob stashed his wife in a secluded house in the woods and constantly cheated on her. Prince was arrogant and condescending. Not counting on a proper four way split of any kind with these pirates I required all the household bills be paid by them and invoked a monthly stipend during their 'occupation'. This was all the money I would receive. My brother never saw a dime.

October of that year at dusk cresting the hill near home, I saw a giant flashlight beaming toward the sky. In the driveway now, said glow was proudly illuminating from the garage roof. The plants had gotten so tall that they'd had to raise the walls and decided to recess a new Phylon roof to augment the elaborate lighting system inside. A good idea unless you forget to reset the electric timer for the day of the fall time change.

Answering my frantic phone call, Bee Bob's disgusted wife said that they were in an orange grove being shot at by some angry drug dealers and she was hoping they wouldn't miss. The garage door locked, I sweated out the next hour until the timer clicked and the lights went out. It was my good fortune that the cop next door was fairly useless at his duties considering the construction site WAS vandalized a few times. Not long after everything had been cleared out, I learned that a few 'friends' from Ithaca were included and discovered one digging up my yard looking for jars of money. I felt betrayed by the whole affair and lost respect for him and everyone I knew to be involved.

FAILING at FAILING

I had a live in boyfriend during these tense times. We were quick to be at odds and my regular floating deepened to problematic so a time consuming job seemed like the ticket. A doctor and a pharmacist in nearby Zephyrhills were opening a restaurant with the hopes of it failing miserably to use as a tax write off.

My knowledge of alcohol had only been gathered internally so far and I had never worked in a bar so naturally they saw me as the perfect fit for bar manager. A 24 year old single mother of two was to run the restaurant and a 17 year old boy was signed on as head chef. We were each put in charge of all aspects of our sections; ordering, hiring, bookkeeping, everything. When one of us needed money they would hand over a signed blank check.

Their problem was that all three of us were completely honest, hardworking people who took pride in making their station the best it could be. For almost a year it was the most popular place in town. Zephyrhills was geared toward the retirement community so we steered the place toward families and daters and offered a night life for both. I had drink specials and turned the volume up on the juke box after the dining room closed. The packed bar was too big for one person and I eventually hired the very capable Dennis to work with me. We had great chemistry and kept the place jumping. I could have ordered cases of wine and liquor for us all, something the owners were banking on, but not once did I ever 'lose track' of a bottle or what money was made each night.

I would almost stake my life on the fact that the 'Chef' they hired is quite an excellent or even famous one somewhere today. He lived for cooking. After the kitchen closed he would come into the bar and order two Tanqueray and tonics. By the time he was closing in on the second one, he was emphatically discussing the many attributes of a well-crafted roasted something or teaching filleting techniques to anyone who would listen. Looking like a blond Joseph Gordon-Levitt, he was as sweet as any dessert he dreamed up and the food he produced was always high quality and innovative for its time.

And because of that, the dining room was generally crowded if not full. The 24 year old Mother/manager was superb at both of those jobs. She ran the dining room with complete efficiency and kept only a competent staff. Drinks came quickly, linen covered tables properly set, warm bread offered, food served hot and delicious, all with smiles and dignity.

The pharmacist and doctor were going out of their minds!

I actually never met the doctor, the pharmacist doing all the negotiating and money transactions. He was a pleasant little fellow out for a good time in life. He married a young blonde sex toy who took full advantage of the bar that plied her with the Kahlua and Cokes she so dearly loved. They were both kind souls though so no one minded their presence. They came in for dinner often, starting their evening off by wandering around behind the scenes with never ending drinks and matching goofy smiles.

My day was a long one and seven days a week but I didn't mind, considering what was at home. I did manage to become pregnant one awful night but soon into it had a miscarriage during prep work time. Mr. Goofy was there alone that day and he led me back to the staff room, settled me on the table with a pillow and blanket and sat with me until things calmed down. He kept a quiet conversation with himself going in a soothing voice. I tuned in on occasion and realized he was talking about his problematic never ending erection. The constant of his voice was comforting so I blocked out the words and let the low tone lull me into a restful state. I worked that night.

They finally had to close down the place as it just wasn't their plan to have it be so successful.

SECTION TWELVE

A SPRITZ OF HOUSE-BE-GONE

I was back in Ithaca when Bob found our last tenants, a couple of college boys who turned the place into a frat house and did their best to demolish it. We ended up having to foreclose, the repairs unaffordable and not worth doing considering the damage that was done.

HOME

No house again, I decided to stay in Ithaca year round. I found myself surrounded by loving, open minded, creative people. I was introduced to Eugene (a lifelong friend) and he hired me on as a helper in his landscape business. I was playing in the dirt again! Upon our first meeting Eugene's face was blown up by a bee sting. My own face had fallen victim to a stinger in the eyelid and was still getting back to normal size. Monsters united!

I took on another job at a restaurant/bar where Bob's girlfriend Jackie worked. There I met a host of new friends, another Jackie being one of them and also a lifelong friend. We began our own brand of raging nonsense at Micawber's a few doors down. 'Work is Fun' owner Mickey was a popular local and his friends filled the bar, including those Handsome Carpenters!

I also managed to fall in with a tight knit group of Bob's friends out in Trumansburg, the tiny village a few miles away from Ithaca with a 'swingin' hot spot', reminding me of the Dade City/ San Ann relationship. This restaurant/bar was called the Rongovian Embassy brought to life by the infamous Alex Brooks and several in this group were on staff. There was a lot of intermingling within these two bars and I'm thrilled to say I'm still friends with most of the people I met in those days. Good cooking and generally living well was (is) the goal. Many of us have chosen to live out in the country

surrounded by the gorgeous and varied landscape the area offers.
Throughout the years, we would celebrate the Holidays together.
Johnny got such a kick out of saying that 50-75 of our closest friends
gathered for Easter at Donnie and Denise's, Thanksgiving at Hitch's,
a Christmas party at the Pryzgocki's and New Year's Day at Scott and
Michael's with Lisa hopping into Scott's wagon for life's wild ride.
Fourth of July, Halloween, Labor Day, Flag Day, Ground Hog's Day,
whatever might be on the calendar; all reason to get together. This
still happens today in altered forms and usually on the smaller scale of
10-20. We're a merry bunch.

My present life continues to grow richer from these friends
and the new ones made regularly. The fabric/upholstery shop that
allows my chosen career provides joy and satisfaction deep in my
bones. Not only do I strive for and often receive a client's 'jaw drop'
from the unexpected new life in their old wooden skeletons, but a
safe atmosphere is provided that invites personal conversation and
I encourage it. I can't tell you how many times I have cried with a
client. A chair redo starts the conversation but the story coils around to
the sick daughter who was nursed in it as a baby or the recently passed
grandfather who read aloud to the grandkids after Sunday dinner.
Someone wants to 'lose themselves' in pretty fabric and a few lightly

directed questions leads to the spilling of a problem they simply can't share with family for whatever reason. In the last few years, college kids have started to wander in clueless as to why. (Could be the Ken dolls beckoning from the display windows.) Listening to their fears and worries of the world can be disconcerting, but I'm happy to report that the job requirements of the higher percentage of these kids are to help the planet's environmental recovery along with finding personal fulfillment. How hopeful is that for the future!?! We all have something that rips at us. Sharing even bits and pieces reduces the gnawing and leaves the spirit lighter, stronger. The world throws us new trials every day. It's easier when the court room is filled with familiar and smiling faces.

Anyone who's met me knows another huge joy provider is my garden. I remember years ago calling out for a home of my own, the stability I so needed, and with the same reoccurring magic in my life I was practically handed my current home on a silver platter. I can't thank you enough, Rudy. I won't bore you with the sense of peace within the walls, but when I'm outside in my yard, I am floating in an entirely different way. It's a full body float, held up by the sweetness of the air, perfumed and colored by the varied life within it. Kneeling to plant alyssum for aroma and bee attraction, I spot the beginnings of last years transplanted Buddleia. It made it! My happiness is to the marrow. That Monarda is spreading out too far. Yay! Time to invite crazily attired dirt diggers over to share the sun, pinch herbs and pull splits gifts. I lift the leaves to expose Hitch's hellebore blooms and the yellow stunners of Katie's tree peonies. Suzanne's ever smiling face still comes to mind from the majestic ostrich ferns and blue black iris' she brought as a house warming present over thirty years ago. Last year, Alice dropped off five buckets of Alpaca poop. I was thrilled beyond measure. The giving and receiving through a garden is done with total abandon. Friendship and other bonds are immediately formed without hesitation. It's hard to be angry or sad in a garden. Oh sure, bugs, deer, leaf mold and a host of other problems abound but then there are those gigantic pink Dahlias, the non-stop Snapdragons with their gift of gab, the Lupines this year my God!, those sweet little allium Mollies, the just picked salad, berries, peas, potatoes and endless other things that override those bothers. There is no place for politics in a garden, too impure these days for the compost. And if you're growing in a beneficial way; organically, native plants, pollinators, etc. you're standing in an area that is helping the planet thrive. You are part of the solution, not the problem here. Patience is learned and Peace is found in a garden. To get lost in the shade changes of a flower is rejuvenating. What a leap forward it is that prisons are starting to have on site gardens tended by the inmates. It's healthier, educational, provides social and working skills and the two aforementioned capital P's. Wow, am I going off! There is always something to talk about in the garden.

I shared these stories and thoughts because they make up the groundwork of my soul. There is a lifetime more, but you get the idea. Our experiences may differ yet the events that form us are likely to have similarities as we are all hanging on by our fingernails to the same spinning rock. With each adventure my own belief system eventually came to stand in cement. I saw that the world would continue to extend both misery and joy and that it was up to me which I would allow to rule my life. It was either Be Happy or Not Be Happy. Focusing on what brought fulfillment rather than stewing in the teardowns seemed the better option and realizing the power of control one gets from embracing the positive made that choice easy. It took a while, but I finally felt the solid ground beneath my feet again. When misery comes, my tool box has ways to deal with it. And when my thorn pullers are misplaced, there are friends to borrow from.

EPILOGUE

A theory says it's an unavoidable fact that you will turn into your parents. I never gave it much intentional thought but I did manage to subconsciously convince myself when I was younger that I would die at Mother's same age of 54. That was until I turned 40 and realized how much life there was left to live. Using that positive thought power, I set about changing my viewpoint.

So…and this is a funny one…at age 54 and almost to the day of her murder, I broke my leg. Permanent knee damage gave me a hampered gate and crooked stance…exactly as my Mother. A clear point for the theory and a big win for the altered viewpoint.

I had no insurance, unable to work for three months and because of that my friends and clients threw not one but two fund raisers in my behalf. Checks poured in, food was brought over and errands were run. I was astounded and can still feel the high from it today. It took me to an entirely new level of solid ground and calm waters. I remember my repeated answer when asked how I was feeling; "I've been to my funeral and it was Fantastic!"

2020 A.D.

ABOUT the AUTHOR

On paper, one might get the impression that Anne is a mild mannered older lady walking among her flowers, cats encircling her feet and a smile of acceptance on her face. She does walk among her flowers as much as possible and Sadie or Bug will no doubt lay her out one day, but anyone who knows Anne would never call her mild mannered, or a lady and her smile is certainly not one of 'acceptance'. Anne is quite passionate about her beliefs of equality, consideration and respect for others, all others, and will tell you about it and anything else on her mind at any given moment, booming it out in her naturally deep voice, emphatic hands waving. Her laughter is frequent and raucous. It's true she does not often sail the seas or travel the Continents, but she takes in deeply whatever joys do come her way. She loves the little things in people that make them unique and yet unites them in the larger picture. What long complicated trail did a person travel to cause that particular stance? Where did that phrasing come from? What caused that scar? She may ask. Anne can be bluntly truthful as skirting the issue is not her nature. Deception is also not in her nature. Comedy is though and getting people to laugh is probably her biggest goal in daily life. Laughter is after all, the best medicine, immediately lightening the load and relieving tensions. So laugh with her. And watch your step!

Made in the USA
Monee, IL
08 November 2020

46871728R00121